LOVE NOTES FROM THE ANIMAL KINGDOM

DR. ALLISON BROWN

PALM AND LOTUS PUBLISHING

Published by Palm and Lotus Publishing

www.palmandlotus.com

ISBN: 979-8-9851252-0-7

For

Comet, Dasher, Oliver, Buddy, and Lily

CONTENTS

Author's Note   vii

Foreword   ix

PART I

1. Introduction   3
2. Love   9
3. Energy   16
4. Health and Healing   29
5. Incarnation   37
6. Death and Reincarnation   50
7. Pain   63
8. Behavior   69
9. Communication   79
10. Animal Siblings   91
11. Bits and Pieces   100

PART II

12. Mac the Squirrel   113
13. Paarthurnax the Betta Fish   126
14. Rooster the Rooster   131
15. Myrtle the Tortoise   136
16. Sasa the Bomb-Sniffing Dog   141
17. A Past Life Healing for Maximus   154

PART III

18. Honeybees   167
19. Wasps   173
20. Whales, Dolphins, and Manatees   178
21. Spiders   185
22. Snakes   190
23. Rats   194
24. Fireflies   199
25. Elephants   204

26. Eagles   209
27. Starfish   215
28. Sharks   220
29. Mosquitos   226
30. Wisdom for Humanity   228
    Afterword   237
    Notes   239

    Pet Participants   241

    Acknowledgments   245
    About the Author   247

AUTHOR'S NOTE

As I engaged in the cover design process for this book, I naturally solicited opinions from friends and family. One cover, in particular, seemed to stand out as a favorite—a simple but elegant design with a giraffe as its "ambassador." An artist friend, whose judgement I trust, confessed, "I like that one, but I'm a bit picky. I would look through the book, expecting to see a chapter about giraffes...and there isn't one."

That makes sense, I thought to myself. But, I really like that cover! Perhaps I should speak to the giraffes—they obviously have something they'd like to say.

What follows is a message to humanity from the Giraffe Collective. Consider it a welcome, of sorts, from their lofty (pun intended) position as Ambassadors to the Animal Kingdom—at least insofar as this book is concerned.

～

Many look upon us because we can see above all that is around us. Physically we can; we can see all that is taking place in our surroundings. But know that no matter your size, you, too, can see around your surroundings. It is not by the need of a long neck to see this. Take [the] time, the quiet, peaceful time, just to quietly observe all that is around you. As you sit and you quietly observe, in time, you will see above all of it. Not just where you physically sit but where you are on your planet. You'll sit and observe it all from a great distance, and you will realize just how small you are and how mighty and grand the planet on which you live is.

As you draw yourself back down to where you sit, with the knowing and the understanding that [life] is greater than you know, you will then have [a broader] perspective of all that's around you, how grand each moment is —each connection, each interaction with others that are around you. You will realize that you are not as small as you were from out beyond where you can see. You are greater than that! Bigger than that! Stronger than that! More knowledgeable than that!

Size does not mean strength. Size is a mere perspective of what is inside. Some of the largest animals upon your planet are the gentlest to be around. We all have our understanding of when to bring our strength out, but it is our gentleness that is around us all the time. It is this that allows others to remain calm and at peace and understand that they have a place alongside us.

Allow your gentleness...allow your gentleness, no matter how big or how small you are, allow your gentleness to be the mirror for those to gather around and see themselves, to look into and sense the gentleness within. It is this gentleness that all animals have. We allow that to be the reflection that others see, so that they can be as gentle as us.

Enjoy every morsel, every minute, for there may never be a time as it is now—to enjoy each leaf, each branch. There's always a new place to look, but it may not be filled with what you are looking for. So enjoy each morsel, each minute that you have. Take your time and enjoy it!

The Giraffe Collective
October 11, 2021

FOREWORD

"What do you mean she can read my mind?" I asked my wife, Candace, as I stood in front of Luna Belle, her gorgeous and currently temperamental Andalusian/Arabian mare. "She knows you want to move her to the other stall, and she doesn't want to go," Candace answered. "But we talked about that before we were even in the barn, and I'm just standing here and haven't even picked up a halter or rope or opened her stall door yet," I protested. "Yeah, I know. Like I said, she can read minds, so if you want to move her, it's a good idea to tell her why and get her permission, so she'll cooperate," she said, "or it's going to be an interesting show!"

This was my introduction into animal communication (a process that I didn't even know existed) and how I found myself silently, with my mind, explaining to a horse why I needed her to move—her grain bucket was going to be in the other stall. Once she "got" the message, she eagerly agreed, instead of pinning her ears back like she had been doing. Hmm...

Just to be transparent, I come from a world where this whole concept is considered pretty "out there," or "woo-woo," as it's sometimes described. I'm a reasonably well-educated man. My early adulthood was spent as a fighter pilot in the United States Air Force. From there, I joined the business world as a serial entrepreneur, running eight different companies over the past thirty years. It would be an understatement to say I'm generally "traditional, left-brained, and analytical" in thought and act, and yet, I've been asked to write a foreword about "talking" with animals. Who'd have thunk it?

There are moments in most lives I suspect, where there occurs a profound moment or two. One of mine came when I observed first-hand, with my very own eyes, that animals can and do respond to telepathic communication. It's hard to believe I just wrote that last sentence, but it's true. Luna Belle was the first but certainly not the last.

I was introduced to Allison and Will by my wife Candace Craw-Goldman. Allison, Will, and Candace are all comfortable in the world of "extra-sensory" communication with guides, angels, past lives, et al. However, Allison and Will's amazing connection to the animal kingdom sets them apart and was very interesting to me, and for some reason, communicating with animals seemed less "woo woo" than conversing with angels.

Maybe it was because we are surrounded by animals at our small farm in rural Kansas, where we are home to a lot of critters, as they say around here. Most found their way to us from the wild or cases of neglect or abuse. By current count there are, in the house or barn, three dogs, eight cats (plus another one who prefers the garage), three horses, a mini donkey named Elvis, six hens, six chicks, and one rooster named Flappy. Plus, there is the actual wildlife that has adopted our farm, and us, as their home...deer, coyote, foxes, snakes, turkeys, possums, raccoons, armadillos, and a whole bunch of purple Martins and barn swallows, in season, a few great Barred owls who appear at dusk most evenings and two hawks...a red-tail we've named Harriet and a very forward Cooper's hawk who patrols, looking for an easy meal. Most recently, we've adopted some honeybees, but I'll get to them shortly.

Through Allison and Will, we've been able to communicate with our animals in ways that are truly astounding. Listening to Allison's skilled guidance and Will's ability to not only hear but speak for the animals we consider family, is something to behold. Their individual personalities come through loud and clear. It was quite profound to hear the "other side of the story" from our animals, who can actually "talk and listen" through Will and communicate with us in a new way. It also gave us the opportunity to ask questions about things we had always wondered. How did you get here? Why here, why us? How did you lose so many teeth? Why do you seem to trust women more than men? To hear the animals actually answer and explain is wondrous!

As you'll see in this book, Allison and Will have done this for lots of people and their beloved animals, and their stories resonate. There is a deep love and tenderness that exists between humans and our animal companions, and how we soothe and heal each other is just now being understood. Our pets' ability to live in the *now* is a lesson for many of us who spend our time lamenting the past or worrying about the future. We have much more to learn from them, I suspect.

To that end, I'll leave you with a short story about the power of *energy* and our universal connection to all "animal collectives" and how that vibration can reach across species and technology to enable and enhance our connection to each other.

As a new beekeeper, I wanted the experience of watching a colony of bees get established in a new hive and grow to be part of our farm family. Last spring, I drove about three hours away, way out in the country, to collect my very first, three-pound "package" of bees. That is ten thousand bees!

I arrived at this guy's property, where there were literally hundreds and hundreds of hives scattered all around. There must have been hundreds of thousands of bees just flying all around, knowing exactly where they were going. But for a novice like me, it was pure chaos—and more than a little intimidating. I drove up the dirt driveway, and this fellow came out to see what I needed. Through a barely open truck window, I told him my name and explained that I'd ordered a "package." He said he'd be right back.

He then returned with a small, thin plywood box, with plastic mesh on two sides. As I watched all the bees flying around the truck, banging into the windows, I realized he wanted to hand me this package through the driver's side window. Through a tiny opening, I asked if he would bring them around to the passenger side and put the package on the floorboard.

Now, this guy was completely unperturbed by the flying honeybee circus going on around him...he wore no protective clothing, no gloves, no netting...nothing. I, on the other hand, was completely freaked out at this point, but somehow (miraculously, in my opinion) no random bees entered the truck when the package was placed inside. The man closed the door, waved good-bye, and I headed out of there.

About a mile down the road, the gravity of the situation began to dawn on me—the fact that there was very little between me and about ten thousand bees. There was just this tiny barrier of a little plastic mesh. And the bees were decidedly NOT happy. You don't realize how loud bees can be when they're displeased and inside a vehicle with you; the energy that came off the package was palpable! I don't know if it was the vibration of the truck or the road noise or what, but there was something about the whole situation that they did not like, and we had three hours to go. I thought about putting them in the back of the truck, but the wind would have likely killed them, and I didn't have any kind of blocking structure to put them in, so I was stuck.

I then recalled something that my wife had said: "If the bees aren't happy leaving there, just play Allison and Will's recording of their discussion with the Bee Collective through the truck speakers; they'll like the energy." I remember thinking, *Yeah, sure...like that will work*. And in the ways of a long-married spouse, promptly, but silently, dismissed it. Now, I wasn't so sure. It was already clear to me that Will has an amazing connection to the animal kingdom—I'd witnessed it myself. Maybe I should give it a try. So, I pulled over, found the YouTube recording, and pressed play. But I had no cell signal. Dang!

I drove on for another half hour, trying to have a calm energy and actually talking to the bees, all the while, frequently looking down to see how many had escaped, because they were not quieting down. I found myself thinking that they were, in fact, getting louder. Finally, I got within cell range, and Allison and Will's Bee Collective channeling began. I kid you not, within about thirty seconds, the bees started to calm—not a little, but a lot! Within about a minute, I could barely hear them, and there was much less movement in the box. I thought, *This is actually working!* That is, until Will started to talk to the wasps and not the bees. Suddenly, the bees started acting upset again...buzzing, vibrating, and moving around much more aggressively.

It was clear that bees do not like hearing from wasps or killer hornets! I quickly hit pause and returned to the beginning of the recording, back to the Bee Collective, and again, the bees quickly calmed down. And so, this is what I did for the next 2.5 hours. I got to listen to Allison and Will on repeat, as their magical connection kept our new colony calm until we could get them in their brand-new hive, where they continue to thrive and appear to be very happy.

Our family has always felt a deep connection to nature and our animal companions. If you, too, feel connected to animals, you will love this book, and I suspect you'll fall for Allison and Will, as well. They are amazing people, gifted and generous and are doing some ground-breaking work in the realm of animal communication. But I also think one of the things you'll take from this book is how talking to animals is not exclusive to them, as skilled and connected as they are. Nature and our own family pets are actually keen to talk to all of us and in fact, are probably already doing so. We just have to learn how to pay attention and be open to trying. Allison and Will are trailblazers, showing us with *Love Notes from the Animal Kingdom* that a whole new, exciting world of connecting with our animals is at hand.

Tom Goldman
Husband, Father, Grandfather, Animal Dad

PART I

INTRODUCTION

Yes...the bond with the humans. You have to understand, all animals have a particular bond with their humans, and it's deeper than you would imagine. They are deeply, energetically connected with whatever animal they have around them, even though they don't understand what it means to be energetically connected. That is the whole reason why they bring animals into their house. There is some energy that tells them, "I must get an animal!" A dog, a cat, a bird, a rabbit, a horse...whatever the animal might be, it is this energetic connection that they've always had. That's why they understand each other. Bucks Arrow, Thoroughbred gelding, age 11

The sacred bond between people and their pets is immeasurable. It is a relationship that transcends time and space...one that is not defined by age, gender, nationality, or economic status—not even your pet preference. Cat or cockatiel, dog or donkey, turtle or tarantula—our pets serve as God's humble ambassadors, modeling unconditional love and sharing that love in a way that not only brings us joy but helps us heal. Many folks even admit to preferring the company of their pets to that of other people! After all, animals are great listeners, they don't talk back, and they really don't demand much of us other than a warm bed, good food, clean water, and our love.

The affinity we have for our pets is born out in the numbers. According to the American Pet Products Association (APPA), almost eighty-five million households have a pet. The APPA states that pet ownership[1] has increased from 56 percent to 68 percent over the past thirty years. And there is every reason to believe that this number will continue to climb, as younger generations embrace pet companionship at even greater rates (62 percent) than their baby boomer parents (32 percent). Not only are we bringing more pets into our homes, we are spending much more on their care. In 2020, the United States pet industry was on track to take in an estimated 99 billion dollars, up from 95.7 billion dollars in 2019!

Although we know that animals have taken on different roles throughout human history, it is difficult to pinpoint exactly when "pets" came into being. Pets, by definition, are animals that are kept for pleasure and companionship, having been tamed and domesticated (adapted for human use) over time. Researchers have determined through archaeological records that dogs were the first animal to be domesticated roughly fourteen thousand years ago, followed by all sorts of other animals, including horses, pigs, chickens, cows, and honeybees. That doesn't necessarily mean that dogs were the first pets, however. Humans began domesticating animals for a number of reasons, including for work, as a food source, or for their skin or fur. Animals as pets, on the other hand, were seen as more of a luxury—historically, pet owners were those who had an abundance of free time and wealth.

There is evidence that cats were first domesticated around 9,500 years ago, both for companionship and for snake and rodent "management." Cats are quite well-known for their prominent role in ancient Egyptian society, where they were often mummified and placed within the pyramids. In addition, several ancient Egyptian deities—Mafdet, Bastet, and Sekhmet—were depicted as cat-like beings.

The human-animal bond continues to be of great interest to researchers, because as you can see, it provides many clues about the evolution of humanity. Indeed, our relationship with animals continues to evolve. Many people have stopped consuming animals as food, wearing fur is no longer a status symbol, circus animals are being freed, and even zoos and aquatic theme parks are being scrutinized. It is my belief that animals are here to teach us the meaning of unconditional love and to make us better stewards of planet Earth. In many ways, animals are here to save us from ourselves.

A Little Background

Through my husband, Will, a psychic-medium and trance channel, I have had the privilege of communicating with animals of all kinds—those that humans care for as pets (both living and deceased), as well as many others that would be considered "wild." These conversations are possible because Will is able to harmonize his energetic frequency with that of the animal or animal *collective*,[2] allowing them to speak through his voice, a process commonly known as "channeling."

Prior to these animal conversations, we already knew that Will could communicate with other physical (living/embodied) and non-physical (deceased/unembodied) energies, such as ancestors, angels, and spirit guides; he had been assisting folks in this way for several years. But it was only out of a desperate desire to connect with our own pets—one in particular, who was presenting us with a severe behavioral challenge—that we started "experimenting," purposefully attempting to speak with (channel) a living animal. That experience, and its subsequent outcome, is described in more detail in chapter eight. Needless to say, it worked, and we were hooked!

Our very first "client" session was nothing short of incredible! We facili-tated communication for a couple who had adopted five rescue dogs. The human parents watched in astonishment, as each of the dogs' distinct personalities was revealed through Will's voice and mannerisms. We spoke about life, death, love, abuse, and many other weighty topics. We laughed and we cried, and at the end, each of us recognized the significance of these conversations, both for the pet and for the human caretaker. Not only did the animals' words serve as a healing balm to the soul of their human companions, they held nuggets of wisdom that all of humanity could benefit from. These unassuming creatures were amazed and extraordinarily grateful to have had the opportunity to express—in human words—the feelings they had for their family members. Initially, they were flabbergasted to realize that this type of communication could even happen, but they were eager to answer our questions. We knew, right then, that not only were these conversations profoundly healing, they simply had to be shared.

Along the way, it became evident that pets weren't the only animals who had wisdom to share. Coincidently, Will and I had transitioned into a plant-based lifestyle a few months after the pet channelings began, and I wanted to chat with the bees about their honey. Vegans eschew all animal products, including honey, and although we were no longer interested in eating meat or dairy products, I couldn't shake this feeling that honey was different in some way. My sense was that it was a gift to humanity from the bees.[3]

This simple curiosity led to a series of conversations with specific animal *collectives* (many of which we are taught to fear or despise). What we found was not surprising. ALL animals of this planet have a message for humanity—each one plays a critical role for not only *our* existence but for the health and well-being of the entire planet. Humans and animals are intricately connected in a beautiful web of creation; we just need to slow down, interact with these creatures from our heart space, and allow them to teach us.

After countless conversations with those in the animal kingdom, our biggest takeaway is to *live in the now, appreciating each moment of life.*

Although your pets will speak about the past if I ask them, they'd much prefer to chat about the joyful moments within their current experience. Animals don't ruminate on previous disappointments or perceived wrongdoings; consequently, they don't get bogged down in the human emotions of guilt or shame. Likewise, animals don't spend time daydreaming about the future...longing for something "better." On the contrary, your pets have shared that experiencing day to day life with their human companions is an extraordinarily joyful opportunity! It is that overarching message I wish to convey within these pages.

Nuts and Bolts

This book is divided into three parts. In part one, I share heart-warming passages from our pet channelings, painstakingly selected from transcripts and audios compiled over the past two years. The excerpts provided by these amazing animals are then organized into chapters based on common themes that cropped up during our conversations. To house the miscellaneous dialog that didn't seem to fit anywhere else, I created a chapter entitled Bits and Pieces.

The animals you'll hear from in part one include many common pets, such as dogs, cats, and horses. Most of the animals were in a physical body at the time of the conversation; however, a few had already transitioned. You'll notice that after each quoted excerpt there is a descriptor (bio) that provides the animal's name, gender, breed, and age at the time of the conversation. If the pet we spoke with had already transitioned or has since passed, that is also indicated, if known. For your convenience, a master roster of part one participants can be found in the back of the book.

Part two contains actual transcripts of conversations with several unique pets we've connected with. Readers who have bonded with a farm animal or who have, perhaps, adopted a traditionally "wild" animal and wondered about the implications of human intervention in their lives may find these chapters particularly compelling. We also get to hear, first-hand, from a dog who has retired from his bomb-sniffing duties and now enjoys his work as a service animal. (Spoiler alert: He doesn't consider it work!)

You'll be captivated, in part three, as you read the transcripts of our conversations with the larger animal collectives we've connected with, including the one that prompted those conversations—the bees. And although we didn't speak to them directly, I've also included, in this section, some intriguing information about mosquitos that was shared through Will's guides.[4] The final chapter houses an uplifting compilation of wisdom "nuggets," short bits of advice for humanity from our animal friends. Like a silk ribbon that ties the whole package together, the collective voice of the *Animal Kingdom* provides a beautiful closing message in the afterword.

Note: The dialogue spoken by each pet or animal collective holds a specific frequency, in addition to the meaning of the words themselves. To honor the intent and integrity of each message, I edited only where absolutely necessary. Therefore, not all of those passages will be grammatically correct.

This book would not have been possible without the many pet parents who graciously permitted their sessions to be shared in this way. I am deeply appreciative of their support! It is my sincere hope that you enjoy reading these heartfelt words of wisdom as much as I've enjoyed bringing them to you.

2

LOVE

Love is the whole thing. We are only pieces.
—Rumi

Of all the topics covered in this book, I wanted to start with love, because it truly is the most significant concept to convey. It is the first thing your pet wants to talk about when they realize they have a "human" voice, and it is almost always the final message they share before we end the session—this magnitude of love that they feel for their human companion and how much they appreciate the love that is shown to them.

Understand that I do love you so! I am extremely grateful to be in your presence. I'm extremely grateful to be provided for each and every day. You provide all that I need...the comforts of what it is to be here with you. And I will show you, as much as I can, how much I love you back. Odin, male domestic longhair, age 9

I know that you love me! I sense it all the time. I want you to know that I love you so much, and I hope I can give it just a little bit back to you in the way that you show me the love. Lucky, male domestic shorthair, age 8

Thank you for everything you've provided me. The love is always wonderful in this house! Shadow, male Ragdoll, age 18 months

I thank you for everything you've done for me, all the love you've provided, and all the care you've given me. I know I've been a bit of a handful at times, but you always provide that comfort and that love to me. So I thank you for everything you've done! I hope that I'm able to give some of that back to you. Simba, male domestic shorthair, age 13 (since deceased)

I thank you for everything that you've given me and provided for me. You've given me a wonderful home to be in, and I thank you for that. I just want to say how much I do love being part of this family, and I do love you, Mom. I really do! I hope I'm able to show that to you. Louis, male domestic shorthair, age 11

Just continue to show me the love and care that you are, and I'll continue to be by your side and show you the love that I'm here to show you. Huck, male Havachon, age 4 months

Understand that all I want to do is show my love! Macs, male Lab mix, age 9

I love you, I extremely love you! Sage, female white shepherd mix, age 3

It is your love that I require; that is what will uplift me. Always be by my side, as I've been by yours. Griffin, male Irish terrier, age 8

I love you, and I will snuggle next to you always! That's why I'm there. I want to be with you, and I know you want to be with me. Linus, male miniature schnauzer, age 10

I just want to say I love [my parents]. I thank them for allowing me to be in their home. It's been so wonderful! I do enjoy it. They

provide everything for me, and I'm so thankful! Callie, female domestic down hair, age 9

While the *feeling* of love is unmistakable, it is often difficult to convey the depth of our love in words. But it doesn't stop us from trying! Did you know that there have been an estimated *one hundred million* love songs recorded throughout history? Not surprising when we understand that it is the creative expression of this universal love that gives us joy and purpose. Here are just some of the beautiful and unique ways the animals have attempted to express their love and appreciation for their human companions.

I know at times that I'm a bit more than you can handle. My wild side sometimes gets the best of me. But I thank you for all that you've done and all the love that you've provided to me. It's not just when you're around; I sense you all the time. You're pushing that love out all the time, and it's very comforting, and I thank you for that. I hope that I'm able to give that back to you the way you expect I should. I know that as we grow together, that bond will get stronger, but for now, I enjoy everything that you provide for me. Northern Hawk, off-track Thoroughbred gelding, age 7

All animals, they all expect to have love by their humans. So give us the love that we require, and we'll provide you the love, and the nurturing, and the comfort that we provide. We will provide you the entertainment and joy that we are here to provide, as long as you provide the love and the care for us that we require. I thank you for allowing us to be part of your family! Buddy, male fainting goat, age 10 (since deceased)

Thank you for taking me into your home. I do appreciate it. You've provided everything for me. It's always so exciting! There's always something new. I just thank you for allowing me to do this! Tabs, female domestic shorthair, age 10

I'm glad to be part of your family! It's fun; I enjoy it! [We are here] to give you entertainment. To give you love and joy. It was fun to watch you laugh and giggle as we fell over and just laid there on the ground for a bit. It's difficult for us, because we don't quite understand what's going on, but it was fun for you to understand that and see that. Lily, female fainting goat, age 10 (since deceased)

I thank you for being my caregivers, my humans, and allowing me to be present with you and the other cats that you have. It is most enjoyable, thank you! Oliver, male domestic shorthair, age 2

I want to say thank you for all of the things that you do for me all the time! I know that things can be a bit stressful at times, and that's why I'm with you. I want you to just relax, and be comfortable, and enjoy those small, little moments that we have together. I also want to make sure that you understand...sometimes, I don't always show it the way you do, but I want to make sure that you understand how much I do love you! I love everything that you're doing for me! It's such a wonderful thing to be with this family. I do enjoy it! Larry, male mixed breed dog, age 5

Thank you, Mom. I know that there's been some issues lately, but I'm trying to work through those, and I know that you've been providing me all the love and care that I ever needed. I just hope that I'm able to show that back to you in only the way I can and that you understand how much I do love you, and I do appreciate everything you've done for me. It's wonderful to be part of this family! And I think that over time—yes, we'll be around for a long time with each other, because I know that being part of this family has been so special, and I've really, really enjoyed it. Yes, I would love to come back to this family! Delilah, female domestic shorthair, age 13

I love you! I love you both. I hope I've been able to show you as much love as I feel for you. I know you've always shown me as much as you can. Buddy, male Bassett hound, age 12

I thank you for the time you've given me here. I'm so blessed by it, and I understand it. You've provided everything for me, and I hope you understand how much I love and have provided for you. Marcy, female domestic shorthair, age 12 (since deceased)

I do love you, I really do, and I'm so excited that I am finally with you. I do sense your love. I do! It will only grow stronger. And yes, we will grow together, and we'll experience many things, and we'll teach each other what it is to understand all of it. And I thank you! Bucks Arrow, Thoroughbred gelding, age 11

Love is the currency of the Universe. It is literally the glue—the energetic frequency—that binds us all together. Love is why you chose to bring a pet into your home—to receive love from and give love to another living being. And those of us who are parents to multiple pets understand that love is never divided...love is multiplied. Each time we bring a new pet into our home, we realize all over again that there is always more love to give. After all, it comes from an overwhelmingly abundant Source, one that is never depleted! Not surprisingly, our pets are quite sensitive to the *energy* of love.

I love you, and I thank you! I thank you for everything you've done for me and the rest of the family. You have such a warm, wonderful energy. It's always so peaceful, so comforting, so caring. I hope that I'm able to give that in return to you. I do love you, I really do! Jesse, male domestic longhair, age 2

I just want to say thank you, and I love you, Mom! I do love you so much! Please comfort me and be around me. I do enjoy your energy. Griffin, male Irish terrier, age 8

Understand that the amount of love I have for you is only a reflection of all the love that you have inside of yourself. This is for any animal that you bring in, because it is part of you. The energy is all the same! I ask that you don't forget that. Jackie, chocolate Lab, deceased

Thank you for all the care you've given me through all these years. It's been quite a special bond we've had, and I do appreciate that— everything you've provided. I just wish that I'm able to provide you the same type of love that you've provided me all these years, and I know that will continue to grow. But most importantly, I just want to grow up with you, be next to you, enjoy your energy. Thank you! Ronin, male domestic shorthair, age 2

I do love you, and I love your energy already! We've already connected, and it's been so much fun, and I can't wait. It's going to be exciting when we're all together, and we can rub up against each other and try to understand each other. I know it might be difficult at first. Hopefully, Buttercup doesn't become jealous that there's another kitty. But I think our energies are new enough that we're going to get along just fine. April, female domestic shorthair, age 6 months

Thank you for everything you've done! You've prepared a beautiful home for all of us. Your energy is so wonderful. Your love is so comforting. You just want to roll up into it like a big ball and play with it. It's that comfortable! I just want to say I love you, and I hope I've been able to provide my love back to you the way that you expected. Pepper, female domestic shorthair, age 7

I thank you! Thank you for allowing me to be in your presence, allowing my energy to be around you. I am a bit of a handful at

times, but it is getting used to the surroundings that I'm in. I thank you for everything that you're doing for me so far. I know that you'll take care of me. I'll provide you all that you need...all that you know and then some. Bucks Arrow, Thoroughbred gelding, age 11

Thank you for the love and the energy that you provide to me! I know that you're extremely busy in everything that you do, and you're always there for me, and you always provide everything that I need. But most importantly, I want you to know how much I love you and how much I enjoy giving just a bit of my energy to you, to comfort you, to lift you up. And I thank you for being in your home! Lola, female Catahoula leopard, age 16 months

When I look her in the eye like that, it gives me just a little boost of energy, and I get all filled up and happy inside, and it makes me want to run and go do something! Yes, it's like being filled up! Louis, male domestic shorthair, age 11

Yes, love is the most powerful frequency of all. It has the power to heal, to overcome any obstacle, to right any wrong. And it's the energy that bonds us, inextricably, to our pets. Louis, above, sums it up beautifully—it fills us up, making us happy inside! That being said, love is not the only energy that our animals can sense. Curious? Keep reading!

3

ENERGY

When one tugs at a single thing in nature, he finds it attached to the rest of the world.
—John Muir

When reduced to its smallest particles, everything in existence—you, me, our pets, the book in your hands—*everything* is comprised of tiny, vibrating strings of energy, and all of these energetic strings hold information. This is a *very* simplified explanation of what physicists call String Theory. All of this information-carrying energy is contained within an "energetic soup" that we call the Quantum Field (QF). This means that everyone and everything is connected, energetically, within the QF.

Now, we already know from experience that much of the energy that makes up our existence is not detectable with our five senses. This is because energy waves vibrate at specific frequencies, some we can detect and some we can't. For example, we don't see the energy that powers our television, allows for a cell phone call, or cooks our food in the microwave; but, we can't deny that it exists. Some sounds, like a dog whistle, are not picked up by our ears, because they fall outside of the range of frequencies our ears can detect.

Interestingly, humans can often *feel* energy that they might not be able to detect with their five senses. Have you ever walked into a room where an argument had just taken place and felt a heaviness? Perhaps you can somehow sense when a loved one is in trouble or you *know* who is calling before you pick up the phone. In these examples, you are experiencing an energetic connection—thanks to the QF—that you might not otherwise notice with your primary senses.

This energetic connection that weaves itself through all of existence also allows us to communicate...with each other, with our pets...with anything, really. We can simply "tune in" to certain frequencies. (We will discuss this *tuning in* process in much greater detail in chapter nine.) In the last chapter, I shared with you that *love* is the most powerful of all energetic frequencies, and our pets have the ability to sense (or *tune in* to) that love. Animals are much more energetically sensitive than most humans, however, so they can actually detect all sorts of different energies.

[At] times, I'm sitting and I'm just looking at her energy, looking at how it's all changing and flowing around her, which is always so wonderful, because every time, it's just a bit different—a different color, a different flow. It just moves like water. It's so beautiful!
Delilah, female domestic shorthair, age 13

There are many things that I see that you cannot see. All of us see the things that you cannot see. It is our connection to the energies. This is what the difference is between the animals and the humans. You may sense [the energies] in a different way than we do, but we see them. We see the energies. We see it in its form. It doesn't take a form of a physical being, but it is there. It is the energy passing through. It is not harmful, it is not scary. It's just we sense it, we know it, and we speak to it. Shadow, male American Eskimo mix, age 10

When she's in that relaxed place, that comfortable spot where there's really not a thought—it's just, she's comfortable—it's fun to look at the energy around her and watch it change and shift. Sometimes, it's different colors. Sometimes, it moves. [It's] just fun to watch! Rose, female Nebelung, age 11

I guess the biggest difference is this—animals already know their energy. They already understand their energy, and they accept all the energy that they have—the vibrations...everything. For the humans, many of them don't understand it. So it's not to say we're at a much higher frequency. We are a bit higher, we hold a higher frequency, but we all know. We all understand. We all understand our energy and our frequency. Sfakiana, female mixed breed dog, age 10

All animals do [see energies]. It's how we see. Our eye may look similar to yours, but it sees much more—a different, I think you call it, spectrum. We see light and energy differently. So yes, there is always energy fluttering around. You may call it fairies or sprites, I think, and other types of energies that transit through your home. They're around all the time. If you could imagine your room that you're sitting in right now, if you could imagine that everywhere you looked, there was a little twinkle, a little spark, a little flash, and a little trail...that's all different types of energies that are coming and going, always. Ronin, male domestic shorthair, age 2

There's always some kind of energy around everything. It's always moving. It's always going somewhere, doing something, with our family and with our humans. We could sit and watch that all day. It's so wonderful! Louis, male domestic shorthair, age 11

Anytime that the energies change in either one location or all around the planet, the animals usually sense it first, and then our parents and all the other humans sense it. Linus, male miniature schnauzer, age 1 0

Interestingly, cats have shared that, because of the way they are "wired," they are even more energetically sensitive than others in the animal kingdom.

I think it has to do with being cats in other lives.[1] *Yes, because if I were any other animal before coming into this life, I wouldn't quite understand it. But since I've been able to experience it many different times in many different places, I have an understanding of the different energies that are around us all the time.* Shadow, male Ragdoll, age 1 8 months

To understand how we perceive energy, [understanding] how we **see** *energy is probably most important. Other animals, all animals, they all see and sense energy. But we're a bit different...all of the cats, not just the ones that are taken care of by humans, even the ones that are in the wild. We have a different way that we see the energy. It's much more detailed...*

*...Even when our eyes are closed, we can see things. We see movement. It's almost like seeing the outline of things. If a person walks through the room or another animal is there, even with our eyes closed, we still can see it. We see the energy, the pure energy, the essence. So yes, you can say that we work with energy differently. It's just that we're a bit more sensitive and—what's the word—***understanding*** *of the energy...*

...So we're very sensitive to knowing when there's another animal that might be injured or angry. Even when a human is injured or angry, we sense it, and it looks different.[2] *It changes shape. It changes color, and we know now is not a good time to approach, or*

now is a time that we must approach. And yes, if you're sick or injured, or if there's just something bothering you, other animals sense that too, and they'll come up and help with that. But cats, they're just a bit different...

...[All cats] understand that we can open a gateway between us and you and allow that pure energy, the clean energy—the one that is connected to all things—to freely flow between us. That's why you might feel that warmth and comfort when we're around. Other animals, they do the same thing, but it's a bit different. It's not quite as open...

...But we're more of a pure channel of that energy. I think it's just our approach to life. We think things through quite deeply before we do things. We're very methodical, I think would be the word, about what we do. So we understand how to control ourselves and understand how we control the energy that we have access to. Other animals, they're not so controlling of it. They're more playful with it. They're more, I guess—yes, just playful with it. But for cats, all of us, whether we're with a human or out in the wild, we control it differently. We're very aware of what we can do. Briggite, female domestic shorthair, age 9

As we learned in science class, energy can neither be created nor destroyed; it can only change form (First Law of Thermodynamics). What this means is that physical beings continue to hold an energetic presence even after transitioning out of the physical body, and animals are able to sense that energy. If a family member has passed on, for example, your pet will recognize the energy of their loved one when it comes around.[3] Conversely, you may also sense when your deceased pet is close to you or when they leave you "signs."

We leave the signs. Whether she sees them or not, that is her understanding. But we are leaving the signs behind, yes. We gift her things occasionally. We hope that she is seeing what we are leaving. But she also senses us, as we do come to play. We do enjoy the space that she's in. We enjoy the space around her, so we do get close, and we do nuzzle. So I know that she does feel us. Just know that we are always with you. No matter what animal you have had in your existence, we'll always remain with you. Just be open to what you sense and know, because we are there, and we are gifting you with things. Just keep your eyes open. You will see them. Spooky, male domestic shorthair, deceased

I will continue to come to you. I'll make my presence known, and I think now you'll understand who it is. You'll be able to talk to me just a little differently, even though I'm on the other side. I might be able to bring you a little bit more information from that side, too, because now you're connected differently. Understand that just because we've left you physically, doesn't mean we've left you energetically. No, we're still there. Yes, we'll always remain there. Just a part of us. All animals, when they transition, they always leave just a bit behind, so you can remember. You might sense us and see us when we come around the corner, and it's just our energy, just being present with you, just so you know that we haven't completely left. Cookie, female dachshund-Chihuahua mix, deceased

The physical body that I am is much different than the spirit inside. The spirit is always energetic and is always alive. Griffin, male Irish terrier, age 8

You have to understand that just because another animal is passed away or even a human that has passed away, we talk to them all the time. We see them all the time. We see their energies around all the time. They never quite leave. An aspect of them, a bit of them is

always with us, especially the ones who are extremely close to us. We understand that sometimes, the humans don't quite understand this. They don't quite see them. But we see them all the time, as well as many, many other energies that are around your place. You have more than you understand! Luna Belle, Andalusian-Arabian mare, age 13

We don't speak by words. It's just the sensing of their energy. What has to be understood is all energy, it doesn't matter whether it's here in the physical form, like another animal or a human, or if they've transitioned; it's all energy. Just as I can sense someone as they approach, I also sense their energy. Many animals do this. So when [deceased loved ones] are around—and they're not there all the time —but when they come around, I know it's them, and we play in each other's energy, is the best way to say it. We don't necessarily carry on a conversation, but we know. We know that we're together, and we just enjoy each other's energy. Understand that no matter if we're separated by space, our energies are always connected. Pepper, female domestic shorthair, age 7

Anytime a human that's taking care of us transitions, there is a bit of a void of energy that's there. But we also understand on a deeper level, on a bigger level, that the physical form's not there, but her energetic form is still with us. She's still there. She comes around. It's such a comforting energy when it does come around. It comes through every so often, and I'm not sure if the other kitties sense it, but I know. I see it. Sometimes, she just stands right there, and I like to look and just smile. It's so comforting to know that she's still around. Tabs, female domestic shorthair, age 10

Yes, I do sense [Comet]. She comes around quite often, actually. Sometimes, she comes up and bops me on the nose, just to wake me up out of a sleep. She likes to play. We do talk. It's just energy, though. It's not like we're talking. We just sense each other. We send energy back and forth to each other. It's different. It's a different type of communication. She does all of the stuff she could never do when she was getting older. She wants to play again! It's like she's in a new body. Dasher, male Himalayan, age 13

As Dasher stated above, our pets like to "play" with the energy they encounter. Perhaps you've caught your dog barking into an "empty" corner of your house or pawing at an "invisible" bug. Sometimes, one of our own cats will chase something down the hall, and yet, we see nothing. In many of those cases, your pet could be "playing" with the energy.

I like to play with them and talk to them, and they talk to me. It's a bit of a relationship we have. There's one that comes to visit every so often. Not all the time. I think some of my family have seen it. There's a little ball of energy that darts through the house. I think you would call it, or I think they said, fairy. Little, tiny, little energy. Little tiny, and we just play with each other. I'll stare, I'll run, I'll chase. It's because I'm following it, and we're just having fun! I just see it as a whitish, real white, sparkly, spiky little ball. There's no [specific] time for them. They just come whenever they want. There is one, though, that gets everybody's attention. It's not really visible. It's more like a big wave. What's the best way to say this? It's as if it comes in through the front door and says "I'm here!" And we all look at it, and we all wonder why it's here. And then it just goes and floats through the house, and it's just making the rounds, and then it disappears. It is quite interesting, yes. Shadow, male Ragdoll, age 18 months

I'm not able to detect or understand which one's which. There are so many of them that are there! You have to understand, there's so many; it's almost like a playground! There are energies that come in and out, and a lot of them are, I would think, family. They just want to check in, and then they go on. So I don't know a lot of them, and a lot of them I might know. It's just hard to tell the different energies, because they're all very familiar but, yet, just slightly different. But there's nothing wrong with that. It's quite fun, sometimes! I'll just sit and..."Oh, there's one!" And I'll watch it go through. It's like watching a little ball of energy float through the house. I like the fun of watching it. I don't get too concerned about who it is. Just more that there's this fun energy that comes through the house. Linus, male miniature schnauzer, age 10

I want you to understand, if you could see how we see your home, if you could see the energy in your home the way we see it, I think you'd be amazed! There's always some new energy coming and going, and we love to chase it around, and look at it, and play with it. There's other energy there that's just so wonderful and warm and comforting. There's so much energy in the house! It's all over the place! It's always changing. It's like a big, playful ball, and I like to watch it flow through the house. Tabs, female domestic shorthair, age 10

There's a lot of energy in that house! There are little marbles of energy that roll all over the house, and I like to chase them. It's fun! They're there all the time, but generally, at night, I see more. It's like a little dot of light, and I can chase it all over the place, and we have fun together! It's not any particular type of energy. It's hard to explain. It's not like a human energy, no, and it's not like an animal energy. It's like a little spark! That's about all I can say. It's just a little spark that rolls around the house. It's nothing bad or nothing good. It's just fun to play with! Buttercup, female domestic shorthair, age 1

There's always excitement! There's always something fun and exciting in this family. There's always someone to play with. It's interesting how the energies change, all through the house. Simba, male domestic shorthair, age 13 (since deceased)

Although our pets typically enjoy all of the energies they encounter, on occasion, a specific energy will cause anxiety or apprehension.

I'm not so much frightened of children, it's just that their energy is so much higher than mine—it's kind of sporadic and all over—that I get a little bit frightened by it. I get a little bit scared by it. But some children that have been around before, their energy's a little different, and I don't mind being with them. All animals sense different types of energies. There are [human] energies that come around me that I'm not quite familiar with. I may back away, or I might hide behind someone, but for the most part, I enjoy looking at the energy types that I find that are most interesting. Macs, male Lab mix, age 9

All of your animals have the ability to sense all of the energies that are around. If we enjoy the energy of someone, we'll make our presence known. Some [animals] may be fearful of the humans; but for most, if we sense the energy's a comfortable energy, we will gather around them. We'll intertwine ourselves with your legs, we'll want to get up on your lap...but don't push it! Odin, male domestic longhair, age 9

Another thing our pets are really good at—an ability that this energetic connection assists with—is knowing when their human is on the way home. Your dog might sit on the couch, looking out the window a few minutes before your arrival home from work, or perhaps your cat waits by the front door, meowing, *knowing* that you are about to walk in the door. In many cases, this behavior occurs well before your vehicle can be detected. Lost animals also use this energetic sixth sense to find their way back home, often traveling great distances to do so.

The best way to explain this would be that every animal, including humans, has a certain energy field around them....a "bubble," we'll call it.[4] *The human's bubble is quite close. Sometimes, it's out a little bit farther, but sometimes, it's quite close. For many animals, they push it out quite far...more than you understand. Out beyond the door, maybe down the hallway, outside your building...it goes quite far. It's almost like a sensor. So when our human, our caregiver, our dad or mom, they come in contact with our bubble, we know. "Oh! They're almost here!" And then, that's when we get excited! So that's how we understand.* Paddy, male West Highland white terrier, age 12

Even before she comes to the house, I know she's coming to the house, and I understand that she's going to be there. Yes, I enjoy that! Larry, male mixed breed dog, age 5

She thinks she's [just] driving home, but yet, I know, because she's changed her energy in her car on the way, and I know she's on her way home! You have to understand, the energetic connection between humans and animals goes everywhere. So even if you... hmm...what's the best way to say this? If you took me and you put me somewhere, it's not so much that I'd remember how to get home, but I would remember my mommy's energy, and I'd connect to it, and I'd follow that until I got back home. It's not so much that we remember [how to get home], it's that we connect to the energy, and the energy's like a big, long trail for us—we follow it all the way back home. Pippi, female Chihuahua, age 5

I know they're coming before they know they're coming! Shadow, male Ragdoll, age 18 months

What is interesting is [in] the humans, [the energy field] is quite close to them. It doesn't go out very far. If it does, it's very rare. For the most part, that layer of energy that humans have is quite close, like a tight shirt. But for us, we exude that energy. We push it out as

far as we can. Like I said, all animals do this—this is how another animal senses there's an animal around before they're even seen. It's that energy field that they push out in front of them to say, "I am here. Beware. Be comforted." Bucks Arrow, Thoroughbred gelding, age 11

Sometimes, you might wonder why you sense an animal that's close, and yet you never see them. Or, you see an animal that's in your yard or somewhere out in a field, and they're not looking at you. You try to get close, but you're still quite a distance away, and they stand up, and they still don't see you, but then they run. You have to understand, an animal's energy is out, way beyond yours, [beyond] the human's energy. It's like a big bubble that goes everywhere. It's almost like our ears...out listening, and feeling, and sensing...everywhere! Pippi, female Chihuahua, age 5

Unlike humans, animals don't have a "veil" that separates them from God/Source. They retain their connection with God throughout their lifetime, and therefore, understand themselves as energetic beings (even though they can't communicate that understanding to us). It is that energetic understanding that allows them to see/sense other energies, communicate and play with those energies, and harness their own energy as they fulfill their "assignments."[5] Ultimately, animals understand that we are all united in one gigantic, loving web of creation.

It doesn't matter the size of the animal. We all carry the same energy, the same caring, loving, compassionate energy that we all have. And it's just how we connect with our human. We want to be there. We don't want to be anywhere else. Brandy, female cockatiel, age 7

The energy is what motivates us. [It] is the thread that connects us all! Phoenix, male cocker spaniel, age 13

There are many distractions to pull you away from what is the reality of everything—that you, and all animals, and all things are directly connected to one Source! You have come from the same place. Energetically, you are the same. Physically, you are different. Jackie, chocolate Lab, deceased

There is no veil. [Animals] are directly connected. They are still connected. They are always connected. They have an understanding that you cannot comprehend. That is why they can sense, and see, and interact with all the energies that are around them. That is why they sense, and feel, and know the energy of the humans that are around them, sense and feel the energies of the other animals before they are even present. They understand all of this from that energetic level. There's no need for communication. There is no need for any of it. It is all ONE, and we are all the same existence. Luna Belle, Andalusian-Arabian mare, age 13

[We have] an understanding of how all things are connected, and how all energy is ONE, and how all the information is always flowing from Source and throughout the Universe, and we're always somehow connected. Hâpi-ness, male Egyptian Mau, age 9

The most important thing to remember is that animals don't have a monopoly on this energetic communication. Because we are energetic beings ourselves, connected through the Quantum Field to *all that is*, we, too, have the potential to connect with our pets in this way. My guess is that many of you already do, whether you realize it or not. It all starts in our heart space. And when we learn to communicate with our pets in this way, with our heart energy—through the frequency of love—our relationship with them will flourish!

4

HEALTH AND HEALING

All healing is first a healing of the heart.
—Carl Townsend

There is no question that animals positively affect our health—just ask any pet parent! Studies have found that animals reduce loneliness, boost our mood, and increase feelings of social support. The National Institute of Health reports that animal interaction decreases the stress hormone cortisol and lowers blood pressure, justifying the use of therapy dogs in schools, hospitals, and nursing homes. The National Center for Health Research found that people who had kept a pet within the years studied had the fewest doctor visits, while those who remained pet-less had the most.

Through programs like *Animal Planet, The Dodo,* YouTube, and other video sharing sites, you've no doubt heard the incredible tales of ordinary animals that exhibit extraordinary gifts. Peyo, a 14 year old retired race horse from France makes his own hospital rounds, using an innate ability to find the patients who need him the most.[1] Oscar, a cat who lives in a Providence, Rhode Island hospice center, can somehow identify the patients for whom death is imminent. He strolls into their room and lies down beside them, comforting them through their transition.[2] As remarkable as these animals are, they are not rare—the internet is filled with stories of dogs and cats who can detect cancer or seizures, for example.

One of the most important ways in which our pets contribute to our wellbeing is through the exchange of energy. Do you ever wonder how your pet always seems to know when you are feeling under the weather or maybe just having a bad day? They might lick you in a certain spot or simply lay beside you, providing you with a feeling of comfort while energetically "infusing" you with their own loving, healing energy. But animals don't just "push in" with their positive energy; your pet can also "off-load" your discordant energy and process it through their own body. It is this energetic exchange that enables your pet to remove some of the uncomfortable energy you are experiencing and replace it with pure, loving energy.

That is what they're here for. All animals. They have their missions, but just by nature themselves, that is what they do. It's to transmute, as you call it, because there's always something to take in, absorb, and give back just that much better. Northern Hawk, off-track Thoroughbred gelding, age 7

As any animal that's around a human, we do sense all of the stress, and all of the anxiety, and the fear, and the sadness, and all of the stuff that makes them unhappy. We do our best to help that, relieve that. We'll lay on them, and be next to them, and talk to them. Hâpi-ness, male Egyptian Mau, age 9

Understand that the energy between animals, all animals, and the human is one that is normal. Allow yourself to be connected to all animals...those that you have in your home, surround yourself with the energies. As you surround yourself with these energies, there will be transformation that does take place, because it will all become one energy. It will become one circle of energy. There will be healing, and comfort, and joy all within this circle of energy. Shadow, male American Eskimo mix, age 10

It doesn't matter the dog, we all bring a sense of calm and relaxation to the home. When we snuggle up against you, it's just to pull out any of the stuff that's going on in your day. We have a way of just knowing exactly what's taking place that day, and when we sit there next to you, we're like a big sponge. We pull all that out of you. We don't let it affect us. We just get rid of it. We just don't pay it any attention, but we know that you need to get rid of it to make your day better. So that's what we do. Larry, male mixed breed dog, age 5

I wouldn't necessarily say that we're much higher of a vibration. It's just a very sustained higher vibration. So when you're close, that's why you feel different, and comfortable, and relaxed when you have one of us, or both of us, or whatever animals you have with you, by your side. You can think of it as you're then raising your vibration to meet your animal's vibration. Hâpi-ness, male Egyptian Mau, age 9

I come to you, and I do love on you, and I know your energy changes, and I do enjoy that. I can sense when you do calm a bit. Macs, male Lab mix, age 9

That's why, sometimes, we're a bit persistent when we want to get close to you and curl up with you. We're trying to transfer some of that vibration to you. You can think of us like a big open hole of energy that comes in from all around, everywhere, and we're just putting it into you when you curl up with us. Rose, female Nebelung, age 11

I'm very sensitive to when things change and when things are changing around someone. I know just the appropriate time to be close. What you have to understand is that with any animal, the energy that they put off is very large. Very encompassing. So when we feel that you may be getting sick, when there's something wrong, you're sad, or something's changed, that's when we'll come around more. Or, even if the energy has been changing, we sense that well before you do. So we'll come around just to balance that out just a little bit, make you feel a bit more comfortable. Linus, male miniature schnauzer, age 10

You have to understand that we sense more than just the emotion that you speak of. It's the different shifts in energy and the different things that she's really not sensing yet. It's the energy shifts in her. This is one of the reasons why we're around. We absorb a lot, but we don't take it on. When you're feeling upset, angry, sad, any other emotion, or just your energy's shifting, changing, that's when we like to be with you. We like to take that from you, so you don't have to deal with it anymore. We try to change that energy, move it around, and make it just the opposite of what it was. Rose, female Nebelung, age 11

Not only do animals participate in an ongoing energy exchange with their humans, they are also able to detect specific issues, like illness, disease, or emotional imbalance. They can do this because, as I mentioned earlier, *everything* vibrates at a particular frequency (including illness and disease). And it is this frequency—they often describe it as a light or a glow—that animals are able to detect.

We understand when you're not feeling well....before you even think you're not feeling well. When you get ill or you get injured, especially when you get sick—when a human gets sick, their energies change before they even get sick, and we sense that. And so you might see us come close and snuggle with you, more than we have in the past. It's because we're trying to give you some of our energy to get better, before you even get sick! See, illness or anything with the human body puts off a certain energy. It's like a little light that goes off...a little, um, yes, like a little light that goes off. And we're looking at the light, we're sensing that light, we're sensing the energy of that. So whether that's something inside your body or it's just an illness, it has a particular frequency, a particular light that we see. And we'll go up to it, and we'll make sure you understand that's what we're looking at. We'll put our nose on it. We'll lick it. We'll just tend to it as best as we can, to make sure you understand that there might be something there. Pippi, female Chihuahua, age 5

Each emotion, you have to understand, each emotion that a human has, has a specific energy signature to it, and it gives off a certain frequency and a certain glow that we recognize and we understand. If you are fearful or you are sad, it has a different color, it has a different feel, it has a different look. And we understand when to approach and when not to approach based on this energy. Sully, male labradoodle, age 4

Certain animals are also able to use their sense of smell to detect specific medical issues, particularly dogs.

Yes, it's through energy and also through smell, especially with dogs. Our smell....we can smell things way more than you can, and if you think stuff stinks, you should smell it through our nose! We don't react to [smells] the same way a human does. A human has a peculiar way of reacting to smells. It's very interesting when we see a human smell something, and they don't like it. For us, it's more of...we're looking at it. When we smell it, we "look" at it. It paints a picture for us. Each smell has a different picture, and then we remember that picture, and we understand that the next time we smell that, we know exactly what it is. There isn't a good or a bad smell...they're just smells. Pippi, female Chihuahua, age 5

In many ways, our pets are a reflection of us—they might take on our habits, our behaviors, or our lifestyles. And as complicated as human life can be sometimes, unfortunately, there are occasions when our own physical or emotional challenges have a negative impact on our pets. Luckily, this doesn't happen frequently, according to the pets we've conversed with.

---

*I believe to a certain extent—in a way, we're a reflection of the family we're with. If the family eats a certain way, we're going to eat a certain way. If the family does a certain thing, we're probably going to do a certain thing. So yes, because we're so deeply connected to that family from the time that we're getting ready to be assigned to them, when we **are** connected to them, then we take on the family, the family energy, the family understanding, the family roles—all parts of the family. I guess you could say that we do reflect some of that. If the family is not energetic, then we're probably going to sit around and just be comfortable.* Delilah, female domestic shorthair, age 13

We do our best not to take on the different symptoms, I think you call it, of our family. We do our best to energetically hold that off, and we try to change or transmute that symptom in our family with our energy. But sometimes, it's too much for us to do. We just hold our own, and we hold our space, and we hold our energy. But sometimes, it's just too strong, and it does take over on us. I've had that happen in the past. It's not pleasant, but we understand that we've made that agreement to be with that family for as long as we can be with that family. That's our assignment with them. So we do what we can, and we try to enjoy our life as best as we can. Louis, male domestic shorthair, age 11

Our role there for most of the time is to comfort them and take care of them when they are stressed or when they're injured. It's to give them some of our energy, to take care of them, and to alleviate some of the stress. But sometimes, if it's too much, it's hard to give that much energy without it affecting us. I haven't experienced that, but I would think that if there's that much stress in the family, and there's that much anxiety in the family, and there's nothing we can do about it, it's going to build up in us. And I think it would make us a bit ill, just like it would make the human ill. Delilah, female domestic shorthair, age 13

Although the animals we've spoken with never refer to themselves as *healers,* per se, all animals seem to understand that this ability is just part of who they are.

I think most animals that are brought into a home [with] humans, I think on some level we're all brought there to be healers. We do things differently, each of us. We each have our own specific type of thing we do. Like I said, I do sense when Mom's [had] a rough day or things are going not quite well with her, and I just want to get there and push in and just nudge in with her. It's my way of—oh, I don't know—going into her energy and just changing it. Yes. I think that's the best way to say it. I'm there to change her energy when she's not in that good space. Rose, female Nebelung, age 11

I think [it's] just the true nature of what an animal is, why they're here, and the energy they put off. They don't have to be your pet. They can be the ones that are out in the forest around your home, the ones that run through your yard. You have to understand, if you could see the energy that surrounds an animal, it's so big! It would fill your yard. So just by you being outside and being out in nature, being out in the trees, being out in the forest [with] all the animals that are there, each one of them is casting just a bit of their energy onto you. That's why you feel so relaxed and calm when you go out. Yes, if you want to call them a healer, then I guess that's what you would call them. But [it's] just by virtue of who we are and what we are. That's why we're here. Linus, male miniature schnauzer, age 10

Ok, so animals can help their humans heal, but can they heal themselves?

All bodies, all physical bodies may or may not have physical conditions that are meant to be there, and the ones that are meant to be there are there for a reason. It might be purposeful in [some] way. It also might be purposeful in another, as far as....and this might be difficult, in assisting with the transition. If what is taking place wasn't there to begin with and wasn't there for [a] purpose, but because of circumstances begins to show itself, then yes, energetically yes, that can change. Booboo, male Ragdoll, age 13

I think we can all agree—being around animals simply makes us *feel* better, whether we understand the mechanics behind it or not. Petting our cat, riding our horse, playing catch with our dog, gazing at our fish tank, or talking to our cockatiel provides us with comfort, companionship, and love. It brings us joy! It can lift us out of a funk and help us shift our focus. Connecting with animals, whether at home or in nature, reminds us that we are an integral piece of something so much bigger than ourselves. And ultimately, that is the path of healing...for us and for the planet.

5

INCARNATION

We are all born for love. It is the principle of existence and its only end.
—Benjamin Disraeli

D o you remember when you decided it was time to get a pet? Did you have a "plan?" Perhaps you are an equestrian, with plenty of land, and you were ready to purchase a horse. Or, maybe you love beagles, so when you finally got your own place, you picked out the perfect puppy. Some of you became pet parents "by accident," like a friend of mine, who essentially rescued a goldfish at the end of a wedding —the bride and groom had used goldfish bowls, sadly, as table decorations.

No matter how it happens, whether you adopt a kitten from the animal shelter, purchase a hermit crab from a pet store, or rescue a baby squirrel, it isn't accidental. When a pet incarnates—is born into a physical body— there is a divine orchestration that takes place, and it typically starts with a planning session between the animal and their human prior to either of them incarnating, as described below.

Before I arrived, before I came into this body, and I was just a bundle of energy—I'm a bundle of energy now, too—but when I was not in this body, and before you guys came, we got together, energy to energy, and we agreed. We said we want to play together for a short amount of time while we're here on the planet. So that's what we put into plan, and that's what happened. And that's how that happens. There are always connections being made. There are always agreements, and there are conversations taking place before you're given a body. And then it happens! Pepper, female domestic shorthair, age 7

It's such an interesting thing. When you know it's time, when it's time to come to your family, there's a bit of excitement, and then you arrive, and then you just know because you've already seen everything. You already knew where everything was. You're just part of the family, trying to fit in, trying to get along. That's what it is about, being a family...just finding that right place, a comfortable lap to curl up in. Shadow, male Ragdoll, age 18 months

In order to coordinate your intersection, one of you—either you or your potential pet—will send out an energetic signal, letting the other one know: *"It's time! Time to meet up!"* That's when a connection will be made, and you will bring a new animal into your life. Your pets explain this process as being *assigned* into a particular animal body and then *assigned* to their human.

As you already understand, there is the assignment that we are given...to be with you, this family, in this animal. So it is just that. We know, at a particular point, that it is time. The energy bundle that we are is then cleaved off. It is then brought down into the newborn. It is then brought into existence. We bring forth all of that energy. We are assigned; we are given an assignment to fulfill with a particular family. Luna Belle, Andalusian-Arabian mare, age 13

So think of it as, we're all in waiting, this one energetic group, and we're all waiting for that particular assignment. And we're not sure where we're going to be assigned or what we're going to be assigned. So at the time that we're assigned, then we know whether it's going to be a dog, or a horse, or a fish, or some other large animal or small animal. But once we're assigned, once we know that we are going to be given to a family or brought to the planet as a particular animal, that's when we are a bit excited! Roxie, female morkipoo, age 1

What must be understood by all the humans, for many animals that are in homes with other humans, it's more of an assignment to be there. Macs, male Lab mix, age 9

A better understanding of how this works is that we are assigned to a particular animal, and you have made a call out to the Universe at some point, that you wish to have a dog or some other animal. And then, it is assigned to you of which dog you will have or which animal you will have. Huck, male Havachon, age 4 months

As you are part of all one energy, there isn't necessarily an excitement or lack of excitement. It is the knowing. It is the understanding of everything. You are observing all that is. It is at a particular point, you are then cleaved off, you are broken free, and you know it is your time. That's when the excitement happens! The moment before you enter into that newborn. The moment you enter in is when it is exciting, because you are there, yourself. You are part of everything, but yet you are here physically. And it takes a bit....and you understand where you are. Then it is pure joy, to be here, to be alive...in this body, in this existence, to live this life! Luna Belle, Andalusian-Arabian mare, age 13

You have to understand, it's quite a special thing to be here, to be assigned into a little dog or different animal. It's so exciting when we know that we're coming, because this is a special place. We get to experience all the things that we don't get to experience anywhere else. A lot of times we're just a big ball of energy rolling around, but here, we get to do things, explore things, and just live differently than we normally do. So that's why I'm excited and happy all the time! Linus, male miniature schnauzer, age 10

To understand how we're assigned to a particular family, you have to understand what you as a family have done. You as a family, you have put out into your Universe, into the space you communicate to, that you wish to have a dog. Or, you've put thoughts out that you wanted a dog. And at that point, everything begins to align, and we get the assignment. We understand that we're going to be assigned to a particular family. And once we know we're going to be assigned to that particular family, then it's just a matter of time before this little dog is born. And then, we are brought to you. Roxie, female morkipoo, age 1

This is true for many animals that are on assignment with the humans. It is put out into the, as you would call it, the Universe, or the quantum web, or any other means that you connect to for information. You are then given the information that this is what you should do. You should get a dog, you should get a cat, or get some other type of animal. In this case, you were given the information to get goats. And then, you were led down the information...or led to that information, which led to us. Lily, female fainting goat, age 10 (since deceased)

Sometimes, we get assigned right in. We know exactly who we're going to right away. As we're planning all this, we know the family, and we know the house, and we know everything about it. We send a little signal out, just a little ripple into the Universe, and that family picks up on it. They don't understand why, but they know they have to get another kitty, or another dog, or another animal. And then at that point, the connection is made, and everything's lined up, and there I come! Lucky, male domestic shorthair, age 8

Once I knew that I was going to be there, the alignment takes place. The energies get sent out, they ripple across the Universe, and they find their way to where I am now. There's a sense that this is going to take place. And there I am! Bucks Arrow, Thoroughbred gelding, age 11

Your pets have shared that, especially for first-timers, coming into a physical body can require a bit of adjustment time. After all, they are moving from a state of pure energy, with no restraints or limitations, into a tight, physical container.

At first, yes, it is [difficult] adjusting, with all of the vibrant energy that we have as part of All, the one collective of energy. Then when we're brought into this body, it kind of explodes everywhere, and we get in trouble, or we do things that we're just not sure what we're doing, because [we're] contained. But in time, we adjust to our new body. Now, I do enjoy it, and I hope to come back again and again. This is quite exciting and quite fun! Marcy, female domestic shorthair, age 12 (since deceased)

There are those animals that it is their first time in a physical body. Whether that's a cat, or a dog, or any other animal. Those are usually the ones that are most energetic, because it is something new, something exciting. They surely enjoy that different body, that thing that is just able to run, and jump, and play. And sometimes, they're more difficult to get under control when they're in a home. Others, they come into it a number of times, and when that happens, it is a much more calming energy, because they understand what needs to be in place. They understand that when they enter into a family that it is not appropriate to have so much energy. They're able to just settle into it and be part of the family quite quickly. Griffin, male Irish terrier, age 8

Unlike humans, baby animals are often not born directly into their human families. To link up with you, there are any number of connection points that an animal may take once they incarnate into their physical body. For instance, your pet may have been re-homed, fallen out of a nest, come from a breeder, retired from a racetrack, saved from a puppy mill, or found as a stray. Sometimes, the route your pet takes to get to you is not a straight path. Rather, it has a few detours, as you'll notice in the story of Sasa, the bomb-sniffing dog, introduced in chapter sixteen. But as you'll read about in Sasa's case, the intersection between you and your pet is always beautifully synchronistic...miraculous, really. Your pets understand that it may take some time to finally meet up with their forever family, but when they do, they know it! They recognize your energy immediately.

Understand that when animals come into existence here, and they are an energetic being, they are placed into their body, and it is not determined the family that they are with at that particular point. But at a particular point, they are then turned over to the appropriate family that they are destined to be with. It is not like the humans, where they are placed into a family directly, and that is the family they are associated with. It is almost as if we are waiting for the appropriate family to be ready for us to be accepted into. Sage, female white shepherd mix, age 3

It's interesting. When we're all one big bundle of energy, and it's our time, we get assigned. And even though we get assigned to a temporary home, a temporary family, we know ultimately who our permanent family is going to be. We know their energy. We sense their energy. We've been sending signals out to them to say, "Hey, we're about to come to you. I hope you're ready!" They pick up on those energies, and they say, "Hmm, maybe we should have another kitty." That's where the connection is made. April, female domestic shorthair, age 6 months

We're given an assignment to a particular family. And many times, it's a bit of time before we actually get to that family, but we eventually end up with that family. Roxie, female morkipoo, age 1

It's interesting, because I just remember there was a point where... where I was, I was just getting, um, I say uncomfortable. But it wasn't that things were bad. It was just time for me to go. Yes, it was just time for me to go. And that's when I, then, kind of made that known: "I want to go, I want to be where I'm supposed to be. I want to be with the one I'm supposed to be with." And then, yes, Mom shows up! And I know that's who I'm supposed to be with. Brandy, female cockatiel, age 7

Sometimes, what happens—yes, we are assigned into a body, but we are not assigned to our permanent family, like in this case. Though, as you would say, our first parents took care of us, raised us, but that was just temporary, and we understood that. But we knew we were going to be assigned to this family, and this was our permanent family. Hank, male domestic shorthair, age 7

What you must understand is that not only myself but many animals are brought in and taken care of for a short amount of time. It's a temporary situation. And it is during that time we begin to understand the connection we have with our permanent home, our assignment, as you call it. As we begin to connect, and as we begin to understand that assignment coming on—where we're going to be, who we're going to be with—we energetically push that out. We begin to send it to you. Then, there is that bit of a calling that you sense, and you know that something's about to change. There's going to be a new arrival, there's going to be someone new given to us. And you know that's the one, and when you finally meet, it is as if you already know, because you do! Northern Hawk, off-track Thoroughbred gelding, age 7

That particular assignment may not take place right away. We may be "temporarily" assigned with other humans or left out into nature. But at some point, we are married to our family, our assignment family. Luna Belle, Andalusian-Arabian mare, age 13

Sometimes, it's short; sometimes, it's long. In that case, yes, it's a very similar [process]. We just send out that message. Whenever we're ready to go to the permanent family, we send out the message, and they get it. Lucky, male domestic shorthair, age 8

It's interesting how this works out. We know that we're going to be here. We're going to be in a kitty body, or dog body, or some other animal. But we also know that at some point we're going to go to our permanent family. Sometimes, that happens right from the beginning. Sometimes, when we're with our temporary family, once we're to a point that we know and we understand everything, what's going on, we energetically start calling out, sending that message out there. And then it's received by our permanent family. They get the urge that, "I think we're going to take some more kitties in or take some more dogs in, or some more animals." There's the energetic connection. There's the energetic bond that takes place. Hank, male domestic shorthair, age 7

It's interesting. When an animal—doesn't matter which animal— they know that they're getting ready to either go directly to their permanent home, I guess you would say, or they're getting ready to leave the place where they are now—it's interesting. In this case, I knew it was time. There was something that happened, and I knew it was time. It's like putting mail in the mailbox. You just send it out. You know that your permanent family is waiting for it. They get a sense that it's time. They pick up on maybe the energy of it, or

—I'm not sure, but something in them says, "It's time to get an animal," or "It's time to get a dog, or a cat," or whatever it might be. That's because we've already sent that to you, because we know we're supposed to be with you. And then, everything takes place from there. Larry, male mixed breed dog, age 5

When you're assigned to a family, you're assigned there because of the energy. That's what's most exciting! It's so exciting when you do finally get to that permanent family, and you know that's who you're supposed to be with. You want to spend every moment just snuggled up with it. Cookie, female dachshund-Chihuahua mix, deceased

---

In the case of multiple pets within the same family, occasionally we'll find that the animals planned to come in together. Most of the time, however, when a pet comes into a household, they don't have prior knowledge of the other "sibling's" arrival.[1] Sometimes, animal energies will incarnate at the same time but not necessarily within the same household—a litter of puppies that are then adopted into different families, for instance.

Sometimes, we don't plan to come together. It's two separate connections. When I [knew] I was going to be assigned, I didn't, at that point, know that there was going to be another assignment for someone else, and that's okay. That happens quite frequently, and sometimes, it's a really interesting and joyous thing to have those two connections that are not knowing of each other, because we get to grow together in a much different way. Buttercup, female domestic shorthair, age 1

There are others that I have come in with. There are other energies that I've come in with that you might say are connected. There are other horses that I came in with at the same time. We came here

together, but we were separated. But in a way, we still understand each other's energy, and to some extent, we're still connected. [If we were to meet], we wouldn't recognize each other as the physical horse that we are, but we would definitely understand the energy that we are, for sure. Northern Hawk, off-track Thoroughbred gelding, age 7

Because we love our pets so dearly, we tend to want to give them the best of everything—the highest quality diet, the most exciting toys, or the largest yard, for example. We can beat ourselves up if we feel our pets are not as happy as they could be. Understand, your pets *know* that you belong together—they *love you!* Everything else is simply icing on the cake. Relax!

This is my human! This is the one I'm supposed to be with. Those are all things I think. I think that's a thought and a worry that most humans have about their pets—if they don't provide them a big space, or all the things that they wish to have for them, they're not happy. And that's not true! When we know we're in the right home, and we know we're with the right parents, everything is just fine. It's perfect! I have food, I have water, I have things to play with. I have a big sister. I have love, and that's all that matters! Hâpi-ness, male Egyptian Mau, age 9

In general, yes, we [dogs] enjoy being part of the humans. We enjoy being part of a family. You would call it a pack. We enjoy that! It is part of who we are. There is a part of us that does still understand our wild nature and where we have come from, but we also enjoy what we are receiving. Collective of five dog-siblings: Shadow, Jasmine, Leo, Phoenix, and Sage

Once we are accepted into your circle, into your energy, that is all we have asked. That is all any animal asks. I am yours to bring you

enlightenment and joy. Phoenix, male cocker spaniel, age 13

When animals come into relationship with humans, they are assigned to that individual or family for a reason...a special *mission*, so to speak. Pets call this mission an "assignment." They might be there to comfort a family member through a crisis, to teach about forgiveness, or to help their human develop independence, as was the case with Oliver, our daughter Natalie's cat.

Almost five years ago, Natalie adopted an adorable orange kitten from the humane society. She had recently broken up with her high school boyfriend and was in a slump. She decided that a new kitty would help take her mind off of her sadness. Softies that we are, Will and I agreed. Although Natalie still lived at home, Oliver was to be *her* cat. It quickly became clear to us, however, that Oliver hadn't gotten that message. For example, he was extremely playful (ornery) and was generally too busy for snuggling—he wouldn't allow Natalie to cuddle or hold him for very long. That being said, when Oliver did finally conk out at the end of the day, he typically crashed on his grandparents (Will and me). Naturally, this upset Natalie, because Oliver was *her* cat!

As time went on, Natalie grew into a young adult, doing the things that burgeoning adults do—she got a full time job, enrolled in college, and started dating more. In other words, she became a strong, independent woman and, subsequently, wasn't around the house much. This caused Oliver to bond with us even more, much to Natalie's disappointment. So when we finally chatted with Oliver, during that initial (personal) pet channeling session, we asked him about it. That's when we first learned about assignments; Oliver shared with us that *his* assignment was to teach Natalie to become independent. Had she relied on him too much, she wouldn't have become the self-sufficient person she is today.

Sometimes, the assignments work both ways. For example, in one case, a dog's job was to teach his mom patience, but he soon realized that he had to practice patience, as well. Even wild or stray animals—those that aren't in relationship with humans—come to Earth as part of their own learning process. *All* animals, regardless of any specific mission, come to the planet not only for the embodiment experience itself but also to bring us joy, laughter, healing, comfort, companionship, and of course, unconditional love.

As with all animals that are brought into the human family, we are also there for the love. All animals that are brought into the human family, into the human circle, it doesn't matter whether it is a dog, or a cat, or a bird, or a fish, they all have the unique energy of love that they provide, as well as entertainment, but that is just part of what we are. We are there to provide that entertainment—the love, the joy, the laughter, the fun, and the excitement! Sully, male labradoodle, age 4

All animals do have assignments, yes. Though, if they're placed with humans, it is there for, one, their enjoyment and their entertainment, and the other is to provide just the comfort of the larger animal to be around the human. Buddy, male fainting goat, age 10 (since deceased)

Assignments don't necessarily mean that we have an assignment with a human. Sometimes, these assignments are for ourselves. Periods of lessons for ourselves, as we are in the learning process, as well. If we're left out by ourselves, and we come to be here as...as you call it, a stray (not really a stray—we don't look upon it that way; we look upon it as we have our freedom, and we're able to go where we want, when we want, and do what we want), we [still] have a lesson. Sometimes, we learn that lesson, and sometimes, we don't. But as an assignment, that's what it is—to come here and understand our experience and understand our time here, whether that is with humans or not. Stacy, female domestic shorthair, deceased

The animals we've spoken to have described the incarnation process—
birth—as one of the most joyful occasions of their existence. Coming into
the body and being able to experience *life* in all its forms, whether in relationship to humans or not, is something for which all animals have
immense gratitude. Your pets have also shared that their transition out of
the body—death—is another occasion for joy, as difficult as that may be
for us to comprehend. In the next chapter, the animals themselves
explain why.

6

DEATH AND REINCARNATION

I regret not death. I am going to meet my friends in another world.
—Ludovico Ariosto

B irth, death, and rebirth...the familiar circle of life. It can be both glorious and heartbreaking. We witness life's steadfast progression within nature, as tiny flowers burst forth in spring, bloom in summer, and begin their descent in the fall. By winter, it can feel as though all is lost. But then...without fail...life returns!

Humans, being deeply connected to all of nature, are not impervious to this circle of life and its inevitable transitions. Neither are our pets. However, animals are much less susceptible to the negative emotion that can accompany the transition out of the physical body, the transition we call *death*. That is because, as we learned earlier, animals innately understand that they are energetically connected to the *All*—there is no veil of forgetfulness, as there is with humans. Your pets know that even when they leave their physical body, they never leave *you*—your energetic bond remains. Thus, your pets are not fearful of death, nor do they dwell on that possibility. On the contrary, animals prefer to focus on the *now*, enjoying each day as it comes!

You have to understand that it's a big cycle. We know that our time here is limited. We understand that from the beginning. We're directly connected to it the whole time. We understand. We may not necessarily see the day or the minute that we'll go back, but we understand. We know that each day is a new day, and we enjoy each one, just like we enjoyed the day before. So we enjoy each day, and we don't want you to worry! Linus, male miniature schnauzer, age 10

We don't think about [death] quite like the humans do. It's interesting. Humans, they worry so much about that time. I guess they don't realize what's waiting for them on the other side. But we understand. When that time comes, we're okay with it. We don't worry about it much. To you, it might look like we might be in pain or uncomfortable. In a way, we are, but we don't react to it. We just know it's coming. Larry, male mixed breed dog, age 5

Yes, as disruptive as this is, as painful as it is sometimes, we understand we have a certain period of time for our existence, just as you humans have an understanding that you have a defined period of time that you will be here. But we have an understanding of that when we come in. We understand that it is going to be a short amount of time, or we may be living quite some time. It is just part of our plan. It is just part of our existence. But while we are here, we fulfill each day as if we have many, many more to come! So we don't look upon our end time as it [is] drawing near. We take it day by day, experience by experience, and when that day comes, we understand. Spooky, male domestic shorthair, deceased

When one transitions, the human will hold on to the memories of the physical presence of that particular animal. The memories

begin to fade, but the energetic bond still remains. The memories are to be left behind, but the memories of the energetic connections will grow stronger, and the knowing of the presence will be there. Collective of five pet siblings: Lola, April, Buttercup, Marcy, and Sparky

I do wish to be with you as long as I possibly can. I don't want to leave your place! But I know in time I will have to. And when I do, and when that time comes, I'll be with you after I leave. You'll sense me. Our bond is extremely strong. But once I move on, I'll be in a much better place. Griffin, male Irish terrier, age 8

You have to understand, it doesn't matter the animal, we all understand that we have our limits, our time. It all comes to an end at some point. Brandy, female cockatiel, age 7

We all understand that our time here is limited, and we have to do as much as we can while we're here. It is on a much quicker timeline and scale of time than the humans are here, but we understand what our mission is and what we have to do while we are here. Sully, male labradoodle, age 4

There are two particular points along our journeys that we thoroughly enjoy...it's one, to be assigned again and one, to be released. Though we do enjoy our time while we are with our parents, there's much joy to be had when we are being released and being assigned! While we are there physically with you, no matter how we transition, it's the releasing of our energy, allowing our energy to be released back out, and be collected back up, and then reassigned. Jackie, chocolate Lab, deceased

We understand that, yes, as we get older, our bodies are going to change and be different. Our health might not be the same. But that's okay. That's why we're here—to experience that. We understand that the humans are the same way, and they're here for only a short amount of time, a bit longer than ours. But they seem to think about that endpoint much more than we do, much more than the animals do, and it concerns them quite a bit. We don't think about that. We think about each day. Each day is a new day. We get to do something new! We get to go play; we get to eat something different; we get to see something different; we play with our friends. And then, the next day is the same thing. But then, there is that day that comes that we know we're going to go back and be part of the greater whole of all of it, and then it's all good, because we get to be reunited with all of the energy again and just experience that. What a glorious thing that day is when it comes! So there isn't anything to worry about, but I understand. I just don't want you to worry. It's okay to know that I'm getting older, and I'm going to change. I might slow down a little bit. I might not play as fast as I used to, but that's just part of the process. It's just part of life. Linus, male miniature schnauzer, age 10

Even though our pets do not fear death, that doesn't mean that they are not compassionate to our feelings. They understand that we humans experience profound grief at the loss of a beloved pet. At the same time, however, they want us to remember that where they are going—returning to the *All*—is a marvelous place! They express joy at being reunited with all of their friends, both human and animal, who arrived before them.

I miss being with you! I miss being in your energy. Yes! But where I am, in the existence that I am, the energy that I am, it's much more than I can explain. It is everything that you can imagine and then some! Spooky, male domestic shorthair, deceased

You have to understand, I know that it was a bit difficult for me to leave. But what I want everyone to understand is that just because we've left this body, where before I may have had some issues and some struggles and different things, and there was always a concern, there's no concern! And now, I'm just part of the wonderful All of everything. It's just glorious to be here again! Cookie, female dachshund-Chihuahua mix, deceased

Now that I'm here, and I'm with everyone, it's such a glorious place, such a comforting place! I can do just about anything, as we are all together now. Toby, yellow Lab, deceased

It's quite exciting to be here! This is quite different from everything that I'm used to. I am still [within the] All, part of one collective of wonderful, joyous energy. There is no mission, there is no job. It is a bit of a resetting, a recharging. Filling back up. Just enjoying the wonderful energy that is here, surrounded by All. More than you can understand! Each day there are new arrivals. We get to see them, and it is like a familiar face! The energy is back together. And at some point, yes, we will depart yet again and be reassigned into another animal upon your planet. Until then, though, we just enjoy the moments that we have. The fulfilling energy that is here is just oh so wonderful! Sparky, male English black Lab, deceased

We understand that there is a limited time in the physical existence. And at the moment that the physical existence ceases to be, it is very similar to our entrance in, as we depart that physical existence. There's a bit of joy, there's a bit of happiness, and there's a bit of expectation of what to expect when we are reunited with ONE. But once we are reunited, we are awash with everything that is! It is not [that] we go up and tell stories of what our existence was here. They already know the stories; they already know the existence. So why retell it? You are, then, part of ONE again. The ALL. Waiting to be reassigned. Just enjoying that existence, that energy of ALL! Luna Belle, Andalusian-Arabian mare, age 13

You have to understand, once we are released from the physical aspect of who we were, and we are brought back into the collective of All Energy, everything is a glorious place! It's a wonderful place! It's a very calming and soothing place. It's one that you may not

comprehend. *It's a very warm, relaxing place. It's one place that we would just like to curl up and be with all the time.* Jackie, chocolate Lab, deceased

I know you understand how much I've loved you and how much I enjoyed being with you. And I know that it may have been a bit difficult, but there's something better around the corner! We understand that one day we are all going to transition, but sometimes, it's difficult. In a way, I was quite excited to know that I was going to be reconnected with everything. I wish I could share a bit of that with you. It's so exciting! It's wonderful! There are no words. Cookie, female dachshund-Chihuahua mix, deceased

I miss being with you! I miss being in your energy. I'm so thankful that I was with you for as long as I was. You have provided everything that I ever needed, and I hope that I fulfilled my mission with you, being with you, and providing the comfort and love that I can only provide. But I understand that it is quite different where I am now. It is different to be speaking [like] this, yes. But where I am, in the existence that I am, the energy that I am, it's much more than I can explain! It is everything that you can imagine and then some! [I have] no mission. It is just being part of it All, part of all of the energy, part of all of the one Source. Being collected back up, and being part of this energy, and waiting to be assigned again...

...There are others that I recognize, as well. We all recognize our energies once we've all come back to the one Source. It's a bit of a recharge; it's a bit of a reset. We have left any physicality behind. It is the energetic that is all absorbed back into one. What we have are the memories of what we've experienced, and we understand that through our time here, energetically, we have expended a certain amount, and we are now being fulfilled back up, being ready to be assigned again, fully ready, fully charged. Full of energy! That is why when we come into the new existence, no matter what animal, that is why when you have this new animal, and they are very

young, they're full of energy, just like a newborn baby. Full of energy and full of excitement, as it is all anew. And as we grow older, we settle. We relax. It is as if our energy is being depleted but not in the way you would think. It is just part of the existence. Spooky, male domestic shorthair, deceased

You have to understand that when we're assigned, and we come into a body, that's so exciting! It's an exciting day, because we get to be here. We get to be either by ourselves, which sometimes, we don't like, and sometimes, we get to be with humans. That's the most exciting! And then, the day that we move out of our body, and we go back to that big Source of energy (any existing energy, whether it was here on this planet or any other place; it's all together as one), that's the other exciting day. Not that it's not exciting to be with our humans; it's just...you'll understand. At some point you'll understand what it's like to be reunited with everyone, and not just a few people you remember, but everyone! So when I was reunited with everyone, yes, Spooky's energy was there, but there were many others that I didn't even remember. It's a very glorious place! It's very exciting to be there! Very fulfilling. Now it's just time to relax and enjoy this space before we're reassigned. Stacy, female domestic shorthair, deceased

Our physical body takes some time to get there, but when it's time, and we know it's about to happen, we get a bit excited. We're excited to go back, because at that point, we're back together with everyone! All the humans, all the animals, all the different things. We're all together again as one big energy, and that's where it all starts again. We don't know if we're going to get another assignment or we're just going to stay there. But in time, we find out. So there's a bit of excitement that it's time! Time to go back. Time to go home. Larry, male mixed breed dog, age 5

Now that I'm on the other side, it's interesting to sense [life] differently. It's one thing to experience it while you're in the body

and all the joys of that. But then, when you are out of that body and part of [the All], you look back on it in a whole different way. It feels so much different! Not in a bad way, but in an extremely good way, because you get to sense it from another perspective, and you can see it in all of its different pieces, and how they all fit together, and how they all perfectly combine. Cookie, female dachshund-Chihuahua mix, deceased

---

Many folks seek a pet channeling session when they are faced with a difficult situation. Their pet might be experiencing a serious health issue, for example. Or, perhaps there are end-of-life concerns. Very often, the topic of euthanasia will surface—should we assist our pets or allow them to transition on their own? Naturally, we don't want our pets to suffer. After their death, we might wonder: *Did we do the right thing? Did we wait too long to intervene? Should we have waited longer?* If we are not careful, we can compound our grief with guilt. Be comforted by the fact that your pets understand this existential dilemma, and they trust your decisions. You can't get it wrong.

When it comes to this particular point in the extent of the life cycle of an animal, we will show our understanding that it is time for us to transition. Though it is not comforting to the caregiver that we are with, we will go quietly into a place of acceptance that it is time to move on. We cannot communicate this, but you, as the owner, will understand that there is the point at which it must happen. And there are times that we will transition on our own. There are other times that, yes, you will have to assist us with this, as we cannot communicate where we are. But that is the burden that the owner has taken on...to be the owner of this particular animal. But we honor that, and we honor the presence that we are with you. Collective of five dog-siblings: Shadow, Jasmine, Leo, Phoenix, and Sage

There are times that our human caretakers must assist us, as we need that extra help to transition. Other times, we pass very quickly. Again, it is all part of the divine plan that we have, to be in presence with you humans. Do not take any sorrow in any of this. Spooky, male domestic shorthair, deceased

When it gets to that point, it may not be something I have to say, but [my humans will] just know. They'll understand. But if they don't, I'll make sure that I voice it in a way that they understand. Lucky, male domestic shorthair, age 8

If you sense that it is acceptable to put the animal into a comfortable spot and allow them to transition on their own, then so be it. But if they, in your opinion, seem to be in anguish, then yes, if you must assist, assist—understanding that when an animal is in that state, they do appear to be in anguish, they do appear to be discomforted. But it is their way of settling into their energy and holding their space. They are not in discomfort as much as you would think, but they are ready to transition. They are waiting for you to make the decision. Collective of five dog-siblings: Shadow, Jasmine, Leo, Phoenix, and Sage

You have to understand, so when we're assigned, we give all of our trust and all of our understanding to our human parents. And whatever decisions they make, that's for them to make. We rely on them to make the best decisions. Dasher, male Himalayan, age 13

I would trust my mom and my family. If that's what they wish to do, then I'll honor that and do that. It might be a bit difficult, but if that's what she feels that she should do, then that's what she's to do. Delilah, female domestic shorthair, age 13

I would trust my mom. That's why I'm with this family. Louis, male domestic shorthair, age 11

We've already established that like humans, animals are, at their core, energetic beings having a temporary physical existence. In other words, once the body dies, the soul or energetic essence continues to live on...for example, in the afterlife. But the circle of life doesn't end there. On the contrary, it is a continuous, unstoppable, eternal cycle. What that means is that once your pet is released from the body, and spends a bit of time in the afterlife (reunited with the *All*), it has the opportunity to come back for another physical experience.

Interestingly, our pets don't always come back as the same type of animal. For example, our cat, Oliver (introduced earlier), has a number of dog-like behaviors that we found quite comical. He chases his tail, chews cords (ok, not funny), fetches toys, and actually growls when someone knocks on the door! We have had many cats over the years but none quite like Oliver. We joked to ourselves that he must have been a dog in a prior life, and sure enough, when we spoke to him, indeed he had!

Understand that [after death], we are given another chance. We are given another opportunity to come back around and fulfill another mission, another assignment, just as you will do, as well. Spooky, male domestic shorthair, deceased

No matter the animal or the being, its passing should be one of a glorious time, not a sorrowful time, because it is releasing that energy to be, then, brought back to experience anew. You should be joyful that this energy's allowing itself to come back! Do not be harsh upon yourself. This is purposeful. It's a difficult purpose to understand, we understand this. We get to be here with you, in the physical form, and we enjoy that! We enjoy all of what you've provided for us. We enjoy the times that we've spent together. But each of us understands when it is necessary to transition. Sometimes, this is because of natural causes, natural reasons of the physical being, and other times, it's a very tragic, quick departure. But we understand this is all purposeful. It allows us, then, to

transition into another form. We ask you to sit peacefully with this...
sit comfortably with this and hold the truth of knowing that [the
body] is merely the receptacle for the energy. This is for all things
that are around you. Yes, emotionally it is difficult. That is the
human experience. But it is to be joyful in knowing that the spirit
has been released for another round, another experience. There is
the joy—that is the understanding. That is where the love is held!
Toby, yellow Lab, and Jackie, chocolate Lab, both deceased

Maybe I'll be reassigned one day. Yes, that would be fun! Cookie,
female dachshund-Chihuahua mix, deceased

So when we enter in, and we come into your family, it is as if a
piece of you has been connected. And yes, sometimes, there is a
tragic end, and sometimes, we live to grow as old as you. No matter
the ends, no matter the outcomes, we are all reunited at the end. We
are all brought together, back together, as one. But for most animals,
they're brought back over and over again. Maybe not necessarily to
the same family, as assignments do change. Jackie, chocolate Lab,
deceased

There have been many existences that I've been taken care of by
other humans, and there have been many that I've been on my own.
Each time, I have enjoyed each one of those, yes. Each one is much
different from the other, and I draw upon each of those experiences,
as will my next incarnation. Those experiences are those things that
I will bring forward for just a bit of understanding of how to
interact in the next placement. Spooky, male domestic shorthair,
deceased

I do love you and I do miss you! But remember, I'm there with you.
I will always be there with you, whether I'm in another animal that
you bring into your house or in spirit. I will always provide you
comfort and love and understanding. Jackie, chocolate Lab,
deceased

Have you ever found yourself wondering if your new pet is a reincarnation of an earlier one? Perhaps the kitten you just brought home has the exact same behaviors or personality as a previous pet. The animals we've spoken to have shared that occasionally, they will return to the same family, even if not as the same type of animal. When this unique circumstance occurs, it is typically because there is an agreement made between the human and the animal, similar to the assignments we spoke about in the last chapter. What's more, because the energetic essence is the same, even if it's in a different type of animal body, it's quite possible you'll "recognize" them.

Thank you for everything that you've provided, not only to myself but to Spooky. I thank you for our time with you. It was an honor and a pleasure to be in your presence. We will always be with you in spirit, and who knows? There may be a time that we'll be back with you as another animal, and you'll know it, and you'll sense it. But for now, just know that we are with you, right between your legs. Stacy, female domestic shorthair, deceased

It is possible, yes. That's entirely up to the path that they've chosen. If we have made that agreement along the path to come in more than once, then yes, we'll come in to a family more than once as a different animal. It may not be right away, but it all depends on when that time is to take place and if that agreement has been made. Marcy, female domestic shorthair, age 12 (since deceased)

It does happen, but you have to understand the contractual agreements that have been made with the human. Yes, when the human has been scripting its contract for its existence through its time, it has also contracted with the animal's spirit. It has put in place at particular periods when this interaction will take place, and it may not be the same type of animal, but the spirit is the same. So it may be in the lifetime of one human that that spirit will come through multiple times. When that does [happen], there are particular reasons why this is in place. There are particular lessons that are to be learned by this animal for each of its incarnations. Just as you have one interaction with one animal, you have planned that, as well, and it may be just for the enjoyment of that animal. But typically, if you have that spirit come in over and over, it will be a point of lesson, a point of understanding for each of those intersections, each of those incarnations. I hope this is understandable. Spooky, male domestic shorthair, deceased

I would love to come back to this family, yes! It's hard to say. I know that we had a special bond while we were together. I wonder if it would be just as simple as the intent...connecting that way. If [my family] all collectively just had the intent to say that they would like me, my energy, to be back into another animal, it would be easy that way. [I think they would recognize me, because] I would be able to show it in a way that's almost...when they close their eyes, they would remember exactly what it was like, and it would be my old body that would be in their memory. But yet, in front of them would be a different body. When they closed their eyes, they would sense the same energies. It would all be one! I think, too, it'd be my inquisitiveness. I was always a bit curious about everything. Cookie, female dachshund-Chihuahua mix, deceased

---

Not unlike raising our own children, caring for our furry (and non-furry) friends brings both joy and sadness. Experiencing the death of a pet is one of life's greatest challenges. But their expressions of joy at what awaits them as they complete their journey in the physical body is a comfort to those of us left behind. That knowledge—that our pets are safe and happy—along with the understanding that a part of their energy remains with us, can help to lessen the pain of their physical departure. And the possibility that we might even meet them again when they reincarnate is simply icing on the cake!

7

PAIN

One word will free us of all the weight and pain of life; that word is love.
—Sophocles

The topic of pain is difficult to talk about but so very important. It's nearly impossible to share your life with an animal and not, at some point, worry about whether s/he is in pain. Perhaps you rescued an animal from a traumatic or abusive situation or had to nurture your pet through a surgical or end-of-life procedure. Whether human or animal, pain is an unfortunate part of life.

From the human perspective, pain is a way for the body to provide us with information—don't touch the stove, it hurts! In other words, as unpleasant as it is, the ability to feel pain is a valuable tool; it keeps us safe. Watching our pets experience pain, however, is particularly upsetting, because we take seriously our role as their protector. In the same way we seek to safeguard our own (human) children from distress, we also attempt to inoculate our pets from the discomforts of life.

Although we can't eliminate the possibility that our pets will experience pain at some point during their lives, we can change our perspective about it. All of the animals you will hear from in this chapter have experienced severe pain in one form or another—one puppy experienced a traumatic death; several dogs were rescued from abusive homes; a feral cat suffered injuries as a result of being in the wild; others have experienced the inevitable aches and pains of an aging body.

But as you read their words, you'll come to understand that as energetic beings, animals are able to "compartmentalize" their pain, rather than focusing on it to the point of suffering. As humans, we might liken it to a shaman who can meditate his way into a neutral state, devoid of pain and suffering. The other comforting thing your pets want you to know is that, once they are free from that painful experience, they do not dwell on it. Animals are intensely focused on each *now* moment, enjoying the loving environment they currently abide in. Dwelling on the past or daydreaming about a "better" future are strictly human inclinations—follow your pet's lead and allow them to be your guru.

By all means, continue to provide compassionate comfort and care to your pet when they exhibit signs of pain due to illness or injury. Their physical body needs attention! And regardless of their ability to manage pain, our pets still seek our love and affection, particularly when they are in distress. Although it's easier said than done, your pets simply want to reduce your anxiety when painful events do occur—that is what they want you to take away from this chapter.

Pain is handled much differently with all animals than it is with the humans. We may exhibit pain, as you see it, but inside, we do disconnect from it. We understand it is an energetic [process]. We allow ourselves to disconnect from the pain, to a certain point. It is not always there, right in front of us. This disconnecting of this pain allows our body to try to heal itself, to fix itself. Sometimes, it cannot, but it gives it a chance to do that. The humans have the same capability of being able to shut off the pain and allow the wounds and the hurt to go away. But it is much more difficult, because your mind gets in the way. Jackie, chocolate Lab, deceased

It's hard to describe the exact pain that I'm in, because it's different from what you experience. We understand pain differently. We hold it differently. It is more that we understand that there's a difference between the physical body that we inhabit and the energy that we are...the loving energy that we are. So we have an understanding that is different. It doesn't quite affect us in the same way. But when you see me, and I'm feeling a bit low, and you understand that I may be in pain, it is then that I need the most comfort, the most care. Griffin, male Irish terrier, age 8

Pain for you is something that is an indicator, and it has a certain reflex. For animals, for the majority of animals, when they are in pain, they will exhibit that they're in pain, but it is not necessarily a true indication of how severe the pain is. There is the ability to be injured and have an immediate reflex to the pain, but it is, then, "disconnected," so that the body itself can start to repair and heal. If it remains in the pain state and the reflex state, it has a difficult time healing. So it is disconnected from the pain itself. It does not, as you would think, register with the animal. Now, if you go to the animal and you manipulate or work with the injury, yes, it will inflict some more pain. That is just because you are working with it. You are moving it in a way that it wouldn't normally be moved. But in nature, the animal itself understands the injury... understands the nature of the injury and what it is to heal. And they disconnect from the pain and allow the body to heal the injury. RuRu, female domestic shorthair (feral), age unknown

*Pain is something that is only of, yes, the physical realm that you witness. Pain is not what **you** understand. Pain is something that is expressed through different means. Though I may be in pain, it is overcome by the energy that fills us. It may be that I express my pain in different ways, but what must be understood is that you and* *all those that bring the energy to us, uplift our spirit, uplift our energy and allow us to be in a much better place! It is not like the human; when they are in pain, they express pain in physical ways. We do not express our pain the same way. This is an existence that all animals have. All animals, when they are in pain, they connect to it differently. They express it differently. It is the energy that flows through and in and out of this pain. So it may be that you think that we are in pain, like when we are whimpering, or lying about, or limping, but you must understand that, because we are at a much higher vibrational level, the pain doesn't exist in a physical manner. It is just expressed in a visual manner.* Phoenix, male cocker spaniel, age 13*

Pain is interesting, especially with animals. Pain...how do I describe this? Pain is something that is there, but we don't allow it to be part of our life. We understand it. If we get injured, yes, at that point it hurts, but we can...block it, is the right word. Yes, when it's still sore and tender and something hits it or someone touches it, yes, we may flinch, and it may be sore or look to be sore to them. But we can control our pain quite well. Yes. What also has to be understood is this: If we're in that much pain, if we understand ourselves—and we do, we understand all of the functions of our body—if something is really, truly hurting us, we're going to let our human know. But like I've said, once I'm in pain or it's to that point, they'll know. They'll understand, because I'll make sure they understand. It won't be very dramatic. They'll know. They'll understand. I know that they'll be able to sense my energy at that point. Simba, male domestic shorthair, age 13 (since deceased)*

The next set of messages is specifically intended for those who have adopted animals out of an abusive situation. Your pets want to reiterate that they don't have any desire to dwell upon those days. They want to bask in the love they are receiving now, with *you*, their human parents.

There are things that I wish not to think about. The humans I was with previously didn't take the best care of me, but those are the things that I don't think about. It's better where I am now! I have no need to think about that. It's part of who I am, but it's not what makes me who I am now. It's who takes care of me now and loves me now. That's really what I want to say...it's the love that I'm given now that I truly enjoy! Macs, male Lab mix, age 9

Many of us have had a past, and many of us have had things that are not pleasant. But those are things in the past, and once we are accepted into a home that is of a loving nature, the energy is so much different! There is no need to think about it anymore. No need to think about the things that have happened in the past, because it is what we have here in front of us...what our future is! We don't languish in the past; we stay in the present and look forward to the future. Shadow, male American Eskimo mix, age 10

*It is stuff that does happen. Understand this...for many animals, they may not have had the best circumstances, but once they are brought into a family or around other humans that do cherish them and understand their energy, the memories do fade. All the memories that we have now [are] of what has taken place after that —**that** is what we look upon. We don't tend to want to remember what took place in the past. It's not that we are afraid of it, it's just that it's what we have in front of us and what we love about where we're at now!* Macs, male Lab mix, age 9

These amazing beings also recognize that forming a bond with an abused or feral animal can be challenging; it can take some time for trust to develop. With that in mind, a feral cat gives us a bit of advice.

This would be for all animals that you take in...broaden your circumstances of why you have this animal...broaden your understanding of their energy. Deepen this connection, and provide the space necessary to allow us to come close to you. RuRu, female domestic shorthair (feral), age unknown

As pet parents, there is no way we can completely turn off our emotional response to the pain and suffering our animals experience. After all, that is what defines us as compassionate human beings. We are empathetic to our pets' needs, and we seek to serve them in some small way. It is my hope, however, that after reading their words, you will be better equipped to pause for just a moment and allow a sense of peace and calm to replace some of the fear and worry. When you are able to approach the healing process from that relaxed, heart-centered space, your animal will thrive and your connection will deepen.

8

BEHAVIOR

If your dog doesn't like someone, you probably shouldn't either.
—Jack Canfield

A s any pet lover knows, animals who engage in destructive, dangerous, or disturbing behaviors can be a huge source of frustration for both the human and the pet. In fact, it was an exasperating behavioral issue with one of our own cats that brought about this pet communication process in the first place. Dasher, our thirteen-year-old, almost-blind male had taken to urinating on our beds. Over a period of about 18 months, we tried all sorts of interventions...our local vet, Reiki, and even two pet psychics. Nothing seemed to work. After one particularly stressful weekend, an idea popped into my head. If Will was able to channel *human* energies, why couldn't he also channel *animal* energies? Perhaps we could speak with Dasher directly and ask him for advice. Heck, at that point, we were willing to try just about anything. Needless to say, it worked, and that conversation changed the trajectory of our lives!

We ended up speaking with all three of our cats that day, and it was a profoundly emotional experience. The relationship with our pets became much more intimate after communicating with them in that way. The change in me, personally, was probably the most dramatic outcome, however. I found myself relating to my cats with a greater sense of compassion and understanding. Yes, Dasher's behavior actually did subside for a long while, but perhaps more importantly, I was better equipped to deal with his "accidents" when they occurred.

As with human relationships, when we are truly able to understand why another person behaves the way they do, when we can empathize with their experience, we open the door to not only compassion but forgiveness. And although we love our pets to the moon and back, some of their behaviors can be perplexing...upsetting...maddening. Very often, we simply can't understand the motivation behind the behavior. It remains a mystery, because *we aren't animals*. Animal behaviorists come really close, but let's face it, some of our pets' behaviors may *never* be deciphered. They are simply too complex. For example, even our pets' vocalizations—grunting, barking, whining, purring, howling, and the like—have a variety of meanings.

What you consider a noise is me just vocalizing where I am and how I'm feeling at the moment. It's not necessarily that I'm calling anybody in or calling for someone. I'm just merely vocalizing how I'm feeling at the moment. This is what we do when we're out by ourselves. It allows us to allow others to understand how we're feeling, and those that we're connected with will come around. Those that do not understand who we are and what we are, will stay away. RuRu, female domestic shorthair (feral), age unknown

I just like to talk, so it's my way of...whining is kind of...I don't know. Sometimes, it's just my way of expressing how I feel. It's not that I'm mad or upset. It's a little whine. It's almost like a comfort thing. I don't necessarily mean anything bad by it, but if there's

something that bothers me, I will let you know. Rose, female Nebelung, age 11

For the most part, it's me just saying, "I love you!" It's just kind of my way of being quiet about it. It may seem as if I'm a little irritated, but I'm not. Well, I guess you can say I am, because I can't just say the words. I know what I want to say, because I've heard the words before, but they're not coming out the way I want them to, so they may come out as just a little [grunt] when I want to say something. But that's what I do. I just want to say, "I love [you]!" Linus, male miniature schnauzer, age 10

The grunting. Well, it's a little bit of frustration and just a little bit of...I'm kind of mad at myself. When there's stuff that I don't quite understand, I may grunt a little bit, and it's more me. I just get upset with myself, because there are some things I want to do, and I just can't. But the other one, the snuffing, the kind of [snuffing noises], that's just my way of vocalizing my affection for you! Sometimes, it doesn't come out quite the way I want it. I know it sounds as if I'm angry, but I'm really not. It's more of an affectionate thing that I'm just trying to—I don't want to bark too loud and startle you, so this is maybe like a half-bark. Just a [half-bark], "I love you" kind of thing. Buddy, male Bassett hound, age 12

When I'm barking to you, it's this little bit of a barky-whine kind of thing, I'm trying to tell you, "I love you!" It's difficult to say it in the words you understand, but [those are] my words to say it to you. Sage, female white shepherd mix, age 3

The barking is a type of greeting. We're looking at and seeing the energy of these individuals that come into the home. Sometimes, we recognize the energy, and sometimes, we don't. When we recognize it, we do like to bark, and we do like to greet, in our way. If there is an energy that we're not familiar with, and it is a bit startling, we will have a different bark. But if I don't bark, and I do come up behind, it's that I sense a very good energy, and I want to understand it and be next to it. Sully, male labradoodle, age 4

Many, many cats have a very loud purr, and it means different things to different cats, but for me, it showed how relaxed I really was. I guess you could say it would serve a healing purpose. As everything is vibration, you would then feel that vibration. And if you are connected to a certain vibration, be it the purr or anything else, and it has some healing properties, then yes, you would be healed by it. So if my purr, being as loud as it was and as relaxed as I was, served a healing purpose for you, then I'm honored. Stacy, female domestic shorthair, deceased

---

Several of the cat lovers we've spoken with were nervous about their cat being outdoors. After all, most folks are aware of the trouble cats can get into while hunting, exploring...or just being cats! Although they seem invincible (or maybe just lucky), cats don't really have nine lives; therefore, we worry about them. Interestingly, some cats enjoy the outdoors, while some prefer to stay inside.

You have to understand—and I think this is for all cats—we like to chase things and hunt things. Even though we understand everything's provided for, all of our food's right there for us, it's the instinct thinking. If we see something, it might take us beyond our home. Not that we couldn't find our way back, but there are things out there that I don't necessarily want to experience. Hank, male domestic shorthair, age 7

See, I remember what I was before coming here, because there was a very short amount of time between that life and this life. So a lot of that is still with me. In that other life, I was outside all the time. I wasn't around humans. So I had my...freedom. I think if you spend some time with me, and cuddle with me, and explain that, in time I will understand. I'll do my best to relax a little bit about wanting to be outside all the time. As long as you give me a window to sit in, I'll be able to watch the birds and be able to, in my mind, think I'm chasing them. Buttercup, female domestic shorthair, age 1

Of course, dogs have their opinions about being outside, as well!

There's something about being outside! I like connecting with going outside and just—it's interesting to experience all the things that are outside. I've never had a chance to do that before. Everything is so different! Each thing has its own unique voice, yes. It's so comforting to be outside. Tuna, female corgi-Chihuahua mix, age 15

When it comes to challenging pet behavior, there are several other common themes. Very often, pet parents struggle to understand why their pets don't get along. And of course, pets who act aggressively towards people or other animals are another source of frustration. In many of these situations, the animals explain that it's simply a matter of instinct or energy.

I'm trying to be protective. Protective of the bubble that we're in. I sense their energy, and sometimes, these bigger dogs, they don't mean anything by it, but they put off a very strong—you said aggressive—type of energy. So I'm just responding back. Yes, sometimes, I do act a bit bigger than myself. That's just because I'm trying to protect us. Linus, male miniature schnauzer, age 10

We don't look upon it necessarily as being "mean," although I understand what you mean. But it's not...we don't look at it as being "mean." It's a difference of energy. We read into other animals' energies. We understand their energies. We broadcast our energy, we put it out there. When another animal doesn't quite "like" that energy, their response to it is much different than it would be for another animal. So we don't necessarily look upon it as being mean. It's just their response. And I know, sometimes, another animal may lash out, or bite, or become physical. We understand that. We don't look upon it as being angry or mean. It's just the difference in the energies. And so, once it happens, we back away or are taken out of the situation, and we tend to forget that. But instantly, we do forgive. [We] say, "We understand—you don't like my energy, and I didn't care for yours, and so it's ok. I'll try to remember that and stay away from you." So it's a mutual understanding of each other's energies from that point, because generally, it will only happen once. Pixie, female domestic shorthair, age 2

It's more instinctual. With any animal of like kind, when we're put together, we do have our own personalities, yes. We try to adjust to those personalities, and sometimes that happens. But there is a deeper "thinking," and that would be the instinct that's in all of us. Sometimes, we have to just express our instincts. Especially—how do I say? Especially if we're closer to nature. I'm not sure if that's the right word or not. [Wild], that might be better said, yes. When there are two that have that in them, it doesn't matter if they're inside of a house or outside in the yard. They have that instinct to hold their boundaries. Hâpi-ness, male Egyptian Mau, age 9

At times I'm a bit protective of my house, and yes, I have to show that in a certain way. It's not a way of disrupting things. It's just showing [the new pet] that I still have ownership. I understand now that that's not a good action, the way you've described it. And I understand that, yes, my parents have done what they can. But I believe that understanding that differently, I'll be a bit more relaxed. A bit of it is, I'm a bit anxious at times, and that's the only *way I can show it. So it can be disruptive. Sorry for that. I understand when I do this, and I want to make sure that you understand it's not my displeasure. It's just that I'm making sure others know that this was my house. But now I understand. I know it causes a bit of frustration with my parents, and I just ask them to be a bit more relaxed, because I sense that, and then it sets everything kind of "off," I guess you could say.* Hank, male domestic shorthair, age 7

It's a bit of playfulness. We want to greet the other animal. But we understand that, sometimes, it's not acceptable to just have an outburst of understanding, of agreements between two different animals. It is fun when another animal, another dog, does come around; we understand each other on a certain level, and we must greet each other a certain way. That is just our nature. We do act erratically at times. [When this happens], be with my energy, and bring me aside, sit with my energy to calm it down. There isn't much verbally you must say to me. I understand what I am to do. But be with my energy. Pull me aside a bit and sit with that energy to calm it and relax it. And then, I will be ok. But I may have an outburst again...that is just what we do. Sully, male labradoodle, age 4

Because animals are so responsive to energy, they can tell when the energy their human is exuding doesn't match the words being spoken. When that happens, your pet is going to believe, and react to, the *energetic* communication, rather than the *verbal* communication. In fact, many of the behavior issues our pets exhibit are directly related to the energy that the human is projecting. Unfortunately, it can become a vicious cycle. For example, the more upset we became when Dasher would urinate on the bed, the less likely he was to change, because even if we didn't verbalize it, he could sense the *energy* of our frustration.

Although all animals are energetically sensitive, horses are particularly adept at recognizing when our words don't match our energy.

[Sometimes], there is a slight disconnect between what is being said and what is energetically being given off. This is, sometimes, where the imbalance comes in. You are telling me to be calm; you are telling me to relax, everything is ok. But yet, the energetic reference that is there...what is being exuded does not quite match that. So then it becomes difficult to understand which is greater, and that is where some of my, as you say, willfulness, comes in. Because, I'm not quite sure how to react. What you must understand is that all animals, all humans, all convey a certain amount of energy, and it changes from moment to moment. You look upon it as being a mood, but that mood has a particular energy, and if it's no fun, we don't want to play! Luna Belle, Andalusian-Arabian mare, age 13*

*There is a—call it vibration, or we just call it **ourselves**—that we exist in. And you learn from that. You understand, and you become attuned to it, and as you become attuned to one animal, it is easier to be attuned to another and another. But from an energetic standpoint, it is you connecting with me on a different level, on a different plane. Anytime that you approach, I know you're there. But if this is where the contact and the communication takes place, there's nothing to be said. Just through your energy, you can speak to me. You can open up. You can relax. And in that bit of relaxation, I'll begin to trust. I'll begin to understand what it is you need for me to do. If you're tense, I'm tense. I sense that first. If you could see what tense looks like, you wouldn't go around [it] either! Tense has a different color. Tense has a different shape. It's like a big gray bubble around someone. You see that before you even get to them. You're like, "Ooh, I don't want to go there." So yes, just be relaxed. I would say, though, that if you can reduce your stress, your tenseness* *just a bit, we'll come to an equal balance.* Northern Hawk, off-track Thoroughbred gelding, age 7

Now that you understand that I have this energy field, I ask that you come close, that your energy field be as big and strong as mine. There isn't much you'll need to say as long as your energy is out and surrounding me, from your heart, from your energetic space. We will bond together, we will meld together, and I will calm myself to the point that I will begin to trust, and I will allow you to do the things that you wish. Bucks Arrow, Thoroughbred gelding, age 11

Aside from the common—and usually negative—behavior we've just discussed, animals also express a huge variety of amusing or unusual behavior that their parents are curious about. For example, Hâpi likes to drink out of his mom's water glass. He also preens himself after their cuddle sessions, making it seem as if he wants to "wash off" her kisses.

It's my way of just showing how much I love her. It's kind of like I'm sharing her water, so it means so much more to me that it's her water and not just a common bowl for myself and Rose. It's my way of just being happy and comfortable around her. Hâpi-ness, male Egyptian Mau, age 9

When we preen ourselves and we clean ourselves, it's really just because we're so relaxed at that point, and we just are so comfortable, and it's just our way of showing how comfortable we are. When I get those kisses, I feel so relaxed and so comfortable, and then it's time to just clean ourselves and make ourselves look all pretty, and happy, and beautiful! Hâpi-ness, male Egyptian Mau, age 9

As you can see, animal behavior is a complex but fascinating topic! Just as humans have a variety of personalities and characteristics, our pets are unique, as well. For example, there are any number of reasons a cat might lick its fur or a dog might whimper—there isn't always a common explanation. Sometimes, a particular behavior that we interpret as negative is simply misunderstood, as in the case above, with Hâpi. Adding to the confusion, many seemingly inexplicable animal behaviors stem from pre-domestication ancestry or instinct. What's more, like Buttercup explained earlier, some behaviors are remnants of past lives. As this chapter demonstrates, our pets can be complicated at times, very much like their human counterparts. It's our job as their parents, to simply remain compassionate and seek to understand.

9

COMMUNICATION

My belief is that communication is the best way to create strong relationships.
—Jada Pinkett Smith

If you're a pet parent, I'm willing to bet that at one time or another, you've uttered the following statement: "Gosh, Fido, I wish I could understand what you're saying!" (as Fido barks at you, excitedly). Or, maybe you've found yourself having a full on conversation with your rabbit while she hungrily nibbles on her carrot, staring at you as if you are speaking a foreign language. Oh wait...you are!

Animal behaviorists will tell you to pay more attention to your pet's body language, and they're not wrong. Just like humans, animals use body movement to convey their feelings and desires, very often subtly. But there is an even better way to tune in to your pet. As we touched on in chapter three, we can learn to use our energetic connection to communicate with one another. In fact, our pets are already doing this; it's how animals communicate with each other all the time. Humans just need to catch up!

You also can communicate to me on a much higher level. You have this ability. You can speak with me at a much higher level. You would call it telepathy, and I understand that! Telepathic communication is something that comes in, in a little bit, and it has particular form; it has particular understanding already in it, and then it goes away. It's similar to [the way] I'm speaking to you now. It comes in, and goes away, it comes in, it goes away. And it has a message with it. Sully, male labradoodle, age 4

She has a way of communicating with me. It is that she knows my thoughts, she understands my thoughts, and I understand hers. We do connect like that quite frequently. It is very, very comforting for me. Bucks Arrow, Thoroughbred gelding, age 11

Many animals have this ability. It's one, sensing their energy, and two, if they're able, being able to communicate this way. Communicating without words is what is done most often. It is both ways. They understand me; I understand them. Luna Belle, Andalusian-Arabian mare, age 13

Well, it's interesting, because my mother and I, we speak to each other, but not through words. But it's not always clear. With my grandma, there's a much more clear conversation that takes place. We have a different understanding with each other. It's almost as if we've done this before. We understand each other and know each other that well. Larry, male mixed breed dog, age 5

She may not sense it fully, but we're already doing it. I understand certain things that she's saying. You mentioned speaking without using our voice. Sometimes, I'm just seeing if she can hear me. It's kind of a little game I play, and I like to just give her a thought and see if she responds to it. Sometimes, she does. I don't know if she really realizes she's actually listening to me or not, but she does respond to it, which is quite fun. Delilah, female domestic shorthair, age 13

From an energetic standpoint, all animals, any other animal, we are able to communicate with. Phoenix, male cocker spaniel, age 13

I want you to understand that we've been communicating on a certain level, and I think you already know that. You know my thoughts, and you know what I'm thinking about, and you give it to me right before I'm ready to ask for it. But now, I think that you can hear me. We're going to have much more fun now! Linus, male miniature schnauzer, age 10

With humans it's a little different. It's a different type of energy that we have to connect with. So I'm still getting used to that. I do hear [Dad], and I think he hears me, because sometimes, I do ask questions, and then all of a sudden, there's what I asked for! I'm grateful for that. But sometimes, it's as if I'm not heard, and I think it's just the energy connection. That'll change in time. Buttercup, female domestic shorthair, age 1

That is how we [and] other animals communicate quite frequently. We understand each other's thoughts. We may not always agree with them, and we may have something to say, but that is how most of us communicate. It is most difficult for many humans to do this type of communication. Dogs can sense [your fear], but you can also speak to them through your telepathic means and just allow the dog its peace, and understand that you are saying to it, "I wish you no harm. I wish you the best of peace." And just keep moving, and that dog should be fine. Sully, male labradoodle, age 4

We do communicate [with other animals], but it's not necessarily the same way you would think it's communication. We know of each other's presence, and we know of each other being around. We don't necessarily "talk" to each other, but we do know each other's energy and how close it is. Huck, male Havachon, age 4 months

Yes, we do [communicate with each other]. It's not in a way that you would understand, and it's not in the way that I'm speaking to you

now. It's in a way that is silent. We talk to each other in a way that is....we understand that we're there next to each other, and we're able to communicate. There aren't necessarily words that we can say, but it's just that we know we're there, and we sense each other, and we understand each other's energy. [Telepathically], yes, that would be the word that I was looking for, yes. Delilah, female domestic shorthair, age 11

When we first connect with an animal during a pet channeling session, they are shocked and delighted that we are (finally!) able to understand them. It's endearing to watch the animals process this new experience—speaking through a human voice. Once they comprehend what's happening, however, they quickly grasp the profundity of this type of communication. Without exception, your pets express immense gratitude for the opportunity to connect with you in this way.

Hello Mom! Thank you so much for being here and allowing me to do this! This is quite interesting. It is quite interesting to be present this way. Luna Belle, Andalusian-Arabian mare, age 13

I don't know exactly where I am, but it is a bit different than what I'm used to. Quite intriguing. I'm not quite familiar with what is taking place, but I will become comfortable and more relaxed. This is quite interesting, to be able to speak this way. I understand her when she speaks to me in your voice, but to be able to speak in her voice, in her words, is most intriguing. I thank you for this opportunity! I do. It's very exciting to do this! Bucks Arrow, Thoroughbred gelding, age 11

Hello, Mother. This is wonderful that we're doing this again. It's such an interesting thing. To be so close, yet be in a completely different place. It's very interesting. Shall I say, it's almost as if I'm dreaming. It's almost as if I know that I'm sleeping somewhere, but yet I know that I'm somewhere else doing something else. This is intriguing, and I really like it. This is exciting! Hâpi-ness, male Egyptian Mau, age 9

Yes, it's quite interesting. I'm not sure exactly what's happening, but it's interesting, because I'm here and I'm there, both, and it's quite different. I just want to say thank you! I hope that this will help you understand me a bit better. I know, sometimes, I'm a bit difficult to understand. Larry, male mixed breed dog, age 5

Hello, Mother. This is quite curious. I'm intrigued by what's happening, and I thank you for allowing me to do this. I think it's quite special. I'm not quite sure exactly what's taking place, but I think this is going to be fun! Rose, female Nebelung, age 11

It's quite an experience! I appreciate the opportunity to do this! Huck, male Havachon, age 4 months

This is quite intriguing! This is something I have not experienced before. It is most interesting that I'm not in my "normal" self, and what I'm saying is not what I normally hear....eh, the meow that you would hear. That is my voice that you would normally hear. Yes, it is as if my mother is talking to me or my father is talking to me, and yet, I'm able to speak in the same words. Odin, male domestic longhair, age 9

Thank you for this opportunity to present myself this way. It's quite unique. Yes, it [is] quite pleasurable with the energy that's here. As I was coming here this evening, I already sensed a bit of change taking place. Yes, it was the energy that I was connecting to. Ronin, male domestic shorthair, age 2

[It's exciting], because it's different from what I'm used to! I'm normally playing with my toys, and now, I'm talking in a way that I haven't. Buttercup, female domestic shorthair, age 1

Thank you for this interesting and strange opportunity. I'm not quite sure where I am, but I feel like I'm there, and I'm in a different place, as well. Louis, male domestic shorthair, age 11

It's interesting doing what I'm doing. I'm speaking to you all in a way that I'm not used to, and it's rather exciting for me to do! It's also exciting, because I get to voice the things that I normally get to talk to my mom about, but this is in a way that she will understand. Delilah, female domestic shorthair, age 11

It's rather interesting. I hear a voice, but it isn't what I normally hear. It's....quite different. It is rather strange, but it's quite enjoyable. It's much different than what I'm used to, and I thank you for that. I do love being here with you, in this way. It is quite interesting, and it is most enjoyable that I am able to provide this information. I thank you for allowing me to do this! Sully, male labradoodle, age 4

It's quite different. I want to bark, but it's not coming out as a bark....it's, it's something that I haven't heard before. It is fun, it's intriguing, because I'm not quite sure what's happening. It's different, because....sounds are different. They're extremely different! I thank you for giving me the opportunity to speak to you like this. It is quite intriguing and quite different. Roxie, female morkipoo, age 1

It is interesting. It is different, for sure. I'm used to speaking in my own language and having my needs taken care of, but to speak through someone else is quite interesting. Griffin, male Irish terrier, age 8

It [was] quite an interesting ride on the energy over here! Thank you for allowing me to do this. This is quite interesting and quite fun, actually. I just want to say thank you, again. This is a wonderful experience, and more animals should have the chance to do this! It's quite an energy thing to do. Just as I like to watch the energy float through my house, I feel like I floated through somebody else's house right now. It's quite fun! I think the biggest thing to understand is just all the energy. We're all part of it. You, I, everyone. We're all the same! It doesn't matter. Just the shape is different. Linus, male miniature schnauzer, age 10

It's wonderful to speak with you like this! It's much different than I'm used to. Thank you for allowing me to. It's so wonderful! Briggite, female domestic shorthair, age 9

It's much different than what I'm used to. I hear words. I hear words like my parents, but that's not how I talk! Pepper, female domestic shorthair, age 7

I want to say thank you for doing this. This is quite fun, I will say! The ride over on the energy was quite interesting. Hank, male domestic shorthair, age 7

Yes, this is quite different! I didn't experience this before, and now I'm here. I'm not sure how this is happening, but this is quite interesting. Yes, I recognize the voices. It's different than how I would normally have spoken. Stacy, female domestic shorthair, deceased

---

Before we end each session, the animals we speak with share their excitement about what just took place. Almost without fail, they express their belief that the conversation will positively impact the relationship they have with their human. When we speak to multiple pets in a household, it's amusing to hear them speculate on what will change among the siblings going forward. You see, your animals understand, on a fundamental level, that there was a shift in the *energy* dynamic, one that allowed for communication to take place. And once that happens, it can take the relationship(s) to a whole new level!

I know that having this conversation, this is going to bring on some exciting things, I think! We're going to be able to look at each other just a bit differently now and understand each other so much better. Louis, male domestic shorthair, age 11

I'm appreciative that you've given me this opportunity. Now that we've been able to speak like this, I think that we'll understand each other just a bit differently. We'll connect even stronger, and I think I'll be a bit more relaxed when I'm around you. And I just want to say that this is quite interesting, and I do appreciate the opportunity to do this. Many more animals should have the opportunity to do this! This is quite fun, actually! Northern Hawk, off-track Thoroughbred gelding, age 7

I think that because of this, our energies are going to be just a bit different. We can talk to each other differently, and I think there'll be a little bit different feeling between all of us. I think you'll know me just a bit more. I know I will you. Larry, male mixed breed dog, age 5

Now that we're talking like this, I believe she'll understand me differently. I do enjoy this! This is quite interesting. I know that we do talk to each other, but it's so much different than this. Yes, I think there's going to be—I know there's going to be a big difference in how we approach each other now. Delilah, female domestic shorthair, age 13

I know that we will have a much better understanding of one another. Through this, I have a much greater understanding, and I am thankful, and I am grateful that this took place. Luna Belle, Andalusian-Arabian mare, age 13

You'll be able to understand me closer, now that I've been able to speak with you. I'm thankful that I was able to do this. It was quite interesting! Griffin, male Irish terrier, age 8

I know from this point, I'll try to be just a bit different, because I'm able to talk just a bit differently now, and my thoughts will come through a little bit different. Linus, male miniature schnauzer, age 10

Thank you! Thank you for allowing me to speak to you this way. I'm used to talking to you, but sometimes, I don't think you quite understand. But it is [through] this new voice that I hope that you'll understand me just a little bit better. I thank you for allowing me to do this! It's very unique and different, and I think we'll understand each other just a bit more. Thank you! Buddy, male Bassett hound, age 12

Thank you so much for allowing me to do this. It was quite wonderful! I think that we'll be able to understand ourselves much better now. But I thank you again. This is so lovely to do this, and I thank you for allowing me to do it. Selah, female domestic shorthair, age 6

I think that because we're having these conversations and we're connecting just a bit differently now, I think we'll understand our energies much better. I think we'll look at each other a bit differently, the other brothers and I. We'll look at each other like, "Did you talk to someone? Did you talk to someone?" And I think we'll all agree, and I think we'll share notes. I think overall, yes, just having the ability to talk like this is quite interesting. It's one thing to just normally be around, and be around our humans and purr and meow, but I don't always quite understand it. But now, I think even though we'll meow, there'll be a different connection to it. Let's keep talking! In our own special way, let's just have the conversations like we're having now. I think we'll get along even better, and we'll understand each other even more! I don't know if we can show each other more love, but I think we can. Lucky, male domestic shorthair, age 8

I'm not quite sure what this is, but I thank you for allowing me to do it. It's quite interesting! It's not what I'm used to. It may help all of the energy around everyone change just a little bit, and we can talk to each other differently. I hope that we're able to talk to each other differently now and that we'll understand each other much more. Things will change, I think. It already feels quite different! Simba, male domestic shorthair, age 13 (since deceased)

I hope we're able to talk just a bit differently now, and everybody will understand each other, and we can understand each other from a whole different level. Thank you! Quite an interesting opportunity it is, for sure. Shadow, male Ragdoll, age 18 months

I know that we'll understand each other just a bit more. I know that the energies are going to be a bit different now. I think between all three of us, we're going to understand each other much differently. Maybe just a bit more relaxed. And I do thank you for allowing me to do this, though it is a bit different. Thank you! Thank you for allowing me to do this, even though I'm not sure what I'm doing. Jesse, male domestic longhair, age 2

Anytime you are able to change the aspect of how communication takes place, anytime you're able to change the energy through that communication, it changes the entire dynamic of the entire group, not just us four, but all of us. The energy that was conveyed through the voice, through the words, will carry...will penetrate. This is a wonderful opportunity to be able to speak to you like this. I know that it may be challenging, but understand that we, also, will look at things differently, and we'll begin to shift. It may take some time, but be patient. Collective of four cat siblings: Pixie, Sage, Luna, and Neo

Thank you, Mom. Thank you for allowing me to do this! I think we're going to understand each other much differently now. I know that when I hear your voice now, it's going to be a bit different, and

I think I'll understand the words a little bit better. Rose, female Nebelung, age 11

I want to thank you for everything you've done. You've taken care of me and provided everything that I've wanted. I just thank you for this opportunity. This has been fun! This has been exciting! It's a different type of energy than I'm used to, and I know that we'll have some interesting experiences after this. I know that there'll be a change. There'll be something different across all of the energy now. I think there'll be a different understanding, and I can't wait to see how that turns out! I hope I'm able to provide the love back that [you] have provided to me. I will try! I do enjoy talking like this. It's been fun! Hank, male domestic shorthair, age 7

I just want to say thank you again. This has been interesting and fun. I do feel that the energy's going to change for all of us, if all of us are going to be here speaking. It's going to be interesting to see what happens afterward. I wonder how that's going to be. I guess we'll see! Callie, female domestic down hair, age 9

I just thank you for allowing me to do this. It's been very interesting and quite exciting, actually, now that I'm a bit used to it. And I know that there's going to be a change. I think we're all going to understand each other a bit differently now. Tabs, female domestic shorthair, age 10

I wonder, when this is all over, if we'll understand each other differently. I wonder if we'll be able to communicate differently now? Thank you, Mom. This has been wonderful! Hâpi-ness, male Egyptian Mau, age 9

Again, thank you for this opportunity! It's quite a unique way of being able to express myself. I know that our energies are going to be just slightly different now. I think we'll understand each other just a bit more, and that'll help our relationship grow even stronger. Ronin, male domestic shorthair, age 2

They say that communication takes two—a sender and a receiver—and if either part of that equation is distorted, there can be a breakdown in understanding. Luckily, our pets are here to help us reimagine what that communication can look like. They encourage us to use all of our skills and abilities, even those we've never contemplated, to enrich our relationship with them. With our pets as our guides, we can stretch outside our comfort zone to recognize and acknowledge the energetic core that resides within each of us and then use that energy to communicate in ways we never thought possible!

ANIMAL SIBLINGS

True siblings are bound together by far more essential things than blood.
—Constantina Maud

L et's face it, our pets are very much like children. Heck, for many of us, our pets ARE our children! As such, when we introduce an additional pet into our lives, we often have the same concerns as we do when we bring home a (human) newborn: *Will they get along? Can I love the second one as much as the first? How many is too many?*

Siblings within human families come in a variety of shapes and sizes... adopted children, step-children, birth children, and half-siblings, just to name a few. Irrespective of how they come together, siblings develop a unique bond (even if they don't always get along) that is unlike any other familial relationship. The pets we care for are no different! No matter what type of animal and regardless of whether they live inside or outside, all of your pets consider themselves siblings, just like the humans. Our indoor cats, for example, never physically interacted with our outdoor chickens and goats, but they all knew of one another—there was an energetic bond between them. And when our two goats transitioned, our cats sensed the missing energy.

Because our pets are energetic beings, they really do enjoy having other animals in the home—or on the farm, or in the barn...you get the picture. For them, the more loving energy, the better!

You have to understand, when multiple animals get together, that energy bond that I just spoke of does grow, and we all understand each other from a much different place. It doesn't matter if it's different animals; you get many different animals together, we all understand each other. We all communicate to each other. Spooky, male domestic shorthair, deceased

You have to understand the web of energy that is involved when you have multiple animals in a home. They're all connected. They all do connect! That is why it's always best to have more than one. They do enjoy each other's energies. Understand that it is just the energy. It doesn't quite matter the form that the energy comes in, whether it is a cat or a dog. If we are brought together at a young enough age, the energies are pretty similar, and we will get along very closely as we grow older. It's a bit more difficult as you introduce a new animal, maybe a new cat or a new dog into the family. It is a bit difficult, as those energies are a bit separated. But in time, they will grow together. Griffin, male Irish terrier, age 8

Look at it like a new energy that comes in...a brand new shiny energy that comes into the house. It can only do one thing: brighten the entire place! So when we're feeling a bit slow and old and just want to lay around and relax, that's okay. When that new energy comes in, we might be a little put-off by it at first. But we realize and we understand what that energy is, and it makes us feel just a bit lighter and more comfortable. We may not always want to play, but just by having that energy around, yes, it does make us feel better. Linus, male miniature schnauzer, age 10

Just as the humans have their energy, and their personality, and their understanding, all animals—doesn't matter what animal it is —have the same way of expressing things. They each have their own personality, their own energy. By itself, it will flourish, but only to a certain extent. But when it is combined with other like energies, other animal energies, other human energies, it grows and flourishes more than you would understand. It provides longevity to the existence of that animal. The personalities of the animals are still visible and present, but if you begin to communicate on an energetic level, by whatever means that might be for you, you will begin to see the changes that are in place. But understand, when you bring an animal into your circle, into your energy, you all become one, and there is a deep gratitude from all animals that are intertwined with others. Collective of five dog-siblings: Shadow, Jasmine, Leo, Phoenix, and Sage

I'm not fearful to be alone by myself, but it is always nice to have companions, other animals to be around. When there are other animals around, we can keep each other company. We talk to each other. We comfort each other. Bucks Arrow, Thoroughbred gelding, age 11

As you might have guessed—just like human children—our pets don't always get along. And when that happens, it can be quite upsetting. If you've ever heard two cats express their displeasure with one another, you know what I'm talking about! But no matter what it looks like to us, our pets want us to know that their bond remains strong...and love is the glue.

Well, just as any other siblings, I think we get along. We have our good days, and we have our bad days. But for the most part, yes, I look up to Delilah. Louis, male domestic shorthair, age 11

I love Buddy! He doesn't always enjoy my playfulness. He doesn't enjoy me being so close to him at times. But I do love him, and I understand he loves me, as well. I do like to nuzzle in next to him. He keeps me warm at night. Lily, female fainting goat, age 10 (since deceased)

Rooster's a bit annoying. He gets on my nerves. He's a bit loud. But I understand...it's his purpose. Buddy, male fainting goat, age 10 (since deceased)

It's always nice to have someone else to play with, yes. But I'm not sure if we're going to get in trouble together or not, because that's two of us that can do stuff, and sometimes, that's not such a good thing. Buttercup, female domestic shorthair, age 1

It's an interesting thing to have new energy in the house, where before it was just me. But sharing this energy and understanding and learning from [my siblings] helps me understand the whole relationship we have across everyone in the house. They are each different, but yet very similar. We do get in our bits of mischief. We do like to play a bit rough at times. But for the most part, we understand each other. We give each other space and room. Hank, male domestic shorthair, age 7

I enjoy all the other animals...they're so exciting to be around! There are a few that I don't quite necessarily get along with but it's ok, because we all understand each other's energies. We all understand each other's role. It's always exciting to have multiple pets and energy and all of that around us. It's always fun to play in that energy! Delilah, female domestic shorthair, age 11

Well, it's always interesting. Just when you think you've got everything figured out, and you've got everything planned out, and you've made your home, then there's a new energy that comes in. It's not that it's bad; it's just that it's different. Now, I have to let everyone know that certain areas are my areas, where before it was my house. But now I have to share that space with someone else. At times it is a bit difficult. Hâpi is a bit difficult to understand. I know I've given him some problems, but we'll work it out. It just may take some more time. Think of it as if you had someone new move into your house and you had to share all of your things and all of your space with someone new. It would be a bit tense for a moment, but you would find a way to work around it. Rose, female Nebelung, age 11

Rooster's a bit ornery. I don't much care for him to be around. He's usually in my way, so I try to push him out of the way. And he's a bit loud in the morning, and he does wake us up, but we've gotten used to it. Lily, female fainting goat, age 10 (since deceased)

It's always an interesting place when you have several animals in the house. We all know each other's role, and we know that we all have our own space. Cookie, female dachshund-Chihuahua mix, deceased

---

In an earlier chapter, you read about the energy exchange your pets provide to you—they attempt to remove some of your uncomfortable energy and replace it with pure, loving energy. Well, this gift is not just reserved for humans; animals exchange energy with their siblings, as well. For example, if one animal in your household is sick or elderly, you can be sure the others are conserving their own energy so that they can share it with their sibling. You may have even noticed that once a sick or elderly pet transitions, the others seem to have a bit more strength or vitality. This is because much of their energy was being utilized in support of the weaker sibling. In a similar fashion, when you bring a young pet into a house with older pets, you may find that the juvenile energy invigorates that of the elders.

We know when one is just a bit uncomfortable, and we push our energy over to them to make them just a bit happier. Hank, male domestic shorthair, age 7

Think of it like several different food bowls. You have to divide the food out between the different cats. Well, it's kind of like our energy. We have to divide it up, because we take care of each other energetically. When one's feeling down, we help it feel better by giving it some more energy. When we're not feeling good, or whatever, they're giving us energy. When an animal's ill, like Comet, we were giving her a lot of energy. We were trying to give her a lot of energy, and it was taking a bit from us. Oliver, male domestic shorthair, age 2

Anytime there's an animal that has an extremely high amount of energy, it helps all of the elderly animals that are around. Their energy is being depleted just because of their age, but when there is a young energy that is around, it helps liven us up, rejuvenates us for that little bit and makes us feel like we're a little kitten again. RuRu, female domestic shorthair (feral), age unknown

As we grow old, the younger energy always uplifts us. It's always nice to have some young energy around when we're getting a little bit older. Northern Hawk, off-track Thoroughbred gelding, age 7

There was so much of my energy and a lot of Oliver's energy that was going to just comfort Comet. So it was taking a lot from us and kind of keeping us...um, not as active. Dasher, male Himalayan, age 13

As much as your pets enjoy the company of their siblings, don't feel as if you must rush out and adopt another pet. Your animals understand that it's not always possible to have multiple pets in one home, and they're fine either way. They trust your judgement.

It's always fun to have additional animals in the house. It really is! It's exciting when there's another animal, because each animal has a different energy, and when that energy comes in, it all comes together as one. And it's a really wonderful thing! But I'm just fine without. We all understand when we're given an assignment that we may be the only one, and that is just fine. Roxie, female morkipoo, age 1

It's always nice to have an additional animal energy with us, but we are of an understanding that we are capable of being on our own and handling what we are to handle while we are there. Sully, male labradoodle, age 4

Having another energy, another animal energy, yes, it's always fun! It takes some getting used to, yes, but there's a bond that takes place. There's a different type of understanding that takes place. So it's your choice if you wish to bring in someone that I could get used to and have a nice playmate, sure. But it's entirely your choice. I understand if I'm by myself the entire time, because I do enjoy having the place to myself. Ronin, male domestic shorthair, age 2

The bond between your pets can grow to be incredibly strong. For that reason, it can be difficult for your pet when a sibling dies, even though they have a more complete understanding of the transition process than their human parents do. They don't grieve like we do; that is a human experience. However, they most definitely notice the absence of the physical body and the energy that it held. And like humans, they miss that physical interaction—so much so that, on occasion, they will decide to transition together.

This was the case with our two fainting goats, Buddy and Lily, half-siblings born three months apart. We raised them together on our one acre "farm," where they experienced a long and healthy life. Fainting goats are social animals, and we sometimes worried what might happen if one of them died—would the other suffer from loneliness? Around age ten, Buddy, our larger male, was the first to show signs of aging; he began to have trouble getting up and was moving a bit more slowly. Lily, on the other hand, was the smaller of the two and still quite agile. Even though they were getting older, there were no signs of illness or distress in either of them.

Imagine our shock when, one morning, our son called out to us from the backyard. He had found Buddy and Lily near their sleeping area, both deceased. We searched the yard but could find no signs of a predator, no wounds on their body, and nothing that would indicate they had ingested anything unusual. We were grief-stricken and overcome with the mysterious circumstances surrounding their death. Their passing came a few months after Will had started channeling the animals, so naturally, we wanted to connect with our beloved goats. When we did, Lily explained to us that Buddy had reached the end of his life. Yes, she confirmed, her physical body could have continued, but once she realized he had transitioned, she understood—in that moment—that she couldn't go on without him. They had forged such a bond that it was inconceivable for her to live without her brother.

Although we were shell-shocked and heart-broken to lose them both in one night, we also recognized the blessing in their unusual departure. Being able to grieve them both simultaneously was, we supposed, better than grieving twice. And we no longer had to worry about how one would fare without the other. Of course, we knew, and they confirmed, that they were supremely happy to be reconnected not only with each other but with *all that is*.

Just as two humans come together, and they spend a considerable amount of time together, and understand that they are going to be together for a relationship, it grows much stronger than that. That is just what happens when spirits combine. So as one spirit departs, there is a bit of a breaking that does take place. When that bond is broken, many times—not always, but many times—if it is strong enough, the other will follow, because they want to stay together, bonded in spirit. Spooky, male domestic shorthair, deceased

I want to say that it's been a bit difficult since Cookie has moved on. I feel a bit of a disconnect. But I understand, because I know that this is only temporary, and I know it'll be much better once I'm there, too. Tuna, female corgi-Chihuahua mix, age 15

Yes. I'm sorry for [departing early], but his energy and my energy... we connected so deeply. It was as if we were one piece of energy. When he left, it was sad, and I missed him, yes. So I had to leave. I had to go. Stacy, female domestic shorthair, deceased

As you can see, your pets are deeply connected not only while here in the body but also in the afterlife. Be comforted in this understanding the next time your dogs growl at one another or your cats get into a hissing match. Like their human counterparts, they are just "working it out!" On the energetic level, they are in complete harmony.

BITS AND PIECES

Until one has loved an animal, a part of one's soul remains unawakened.
—Anatole France

As I mentioned in the Introduction, the purpose of this chapter is to house the miscellaneous dialog that didn't seem to fit anywhere else. I felt these excerpts needed to be included—there was too much "good stuff" to just leave it out. In this chapter, you'll find random but fascinating information on a variety of subjects, from a cadre of amazing animals. So, let's dive in!

When animals discuss their past lives, they often share the differences between being an animal in the wild, one in relationship with humans (typically a pet), and a domesticated animal without a permanent home (one that would be considered a stray). They explain that there are pros and cons to each situation; one is not better than the other, because there is learning to be had in each. Here is what one dog had to say:

Being provided for all the time is quite nice, but being able to be free and being able to go wherever I please and choose is also extremely fun and exciting! Macs, male Lab mix, age 9

This next cat lived for many years with a bird sibling. We asked how he navigated that, given the fact that cats and birds have historically been thought of as adversaries.

No animal is an enemy of another animal. Never. But in the wild, what you must understand is that...as you call it, the hunt, is necessary. We look upon it when we're in the wild—I've had many existences where I've been by myself, yes. I have, as you say, [hunted] for many birds and many other animals. But that is to survive. That is for me to survive. So when I am in a different body, a different existence, and I'm being taken care of by a human, and I'm being provided for with all the food I could ever eat and then some, the hunt is still in the background. Some of that does come through. But I understand that I'm in a different place, so it's a bit of playfulness that I will express. And sometimes, yes, in many cases, it could do harm to that bird, yes, or other small animals that you might have. That's more accidental, just because we are bringing forth some of that past life experience. We're wanting to play at that point, yes, because we have all the food that we would ever need. But sometimes, we can't help ourselves but to act in that way. Spooky, male domestic shorthair, deceased

Have you noticed that certain animals have a knack for playing hard and resting even harder? Our cats, for example, love to lie sprawled out in a beam of sunlight that shines in through a window. I've also seen pictures of friends' dogs who have completely taken over their bed! Sometimes, when we see our pets lying around, we might wonder if they are ever bored.

It's not really being bored; I'm comfortable. I've had so many different things that I've done, that it's nice just to relax and enjoy myself. I'm not really bored. I'm just tending to myself. They can play, but if I choose to play, I'll play, and sometimes, I don't, because it's ME time. I want to spend the time for myself. Shadow, male Ragdoll, age 18 months

Bored isn't necessarily the right word, I don't think. I enjoy my time. If you wish, I can be around you much more and be a bit more active, if that's what you're wanting. But I like my time. I like just knowing that you're in the house, and when I know that you're in the house, I relax myself. And I know that [you're] just there, right around the corner, and I can go see [you] anytime I wish. I don't have to be right there with [you] right at the moment. So I can just be myself. Larry, male mixed breed dog, age 5

To me, horses are magnificent animals. They are deeply insightful but also quite imposing. They know themselves, and they know us...so there's no pretending with horses. As any horse aficionado understands, a horse isn't going to do what a horse doesn't want to do. That being said, we can learn a lot from horses—they teach us how to manage expectations, collaborate with the strong-willed (whether human or animal), and practice patience. Without fail, when I speak to a horse, I know we will tackle some deep concepts, as you'll read in the next passage. This horse spoke to us about our relationship with Mother Earth and her evolution.

Any animal that is here now, any being that is here now, is all part of your, as you say, Great Awakening. It is just being in tune with

your planet, with Mother Nature. It is being in tune with that energy. It's how that energy transfers. Mother Earth itself is shifting. The energy in Mother Earth is shifting. There's so much going on! We sense it, and we understand it, so we take in a little bit, and we change it, we transform it, and then we give it back to Mother Earth. It's the same when we do this animal to animal, or human to animal, or animal to human. We take it in, and we change it, and we give it back just a little bit different, a little bit higher, a little bit cleaner, and it tends to help the overall aspect of what is taking place. Northern Hawk, off-track Thoroughbred gelding, age 7

This next pup also spoke about the changes happening on the planet and why the animals are more easily able to sense those changes. She then explained what we humans can do to assist with the evolution.

All animals, and not just the ones that you have in your home, but all animals on this planet...their energy's already very high. Their frequency is already pretty high. They're already deeply connected to the planet, deeply connected to Mother Earth, as you call her. We communicate back and forth in our own way, through our own frequency. When there are certain things that are going on, around the planet or in our area, where we live or where other animals are, we sense; we know; we understand that there are changes [happening] on the planet. We will spend just a little bit of time comforting and just relaxing into Mother Earth, just being there... providing that energy back. You say that the humans are sensing it differently. That's because they're a little bit...um...different... physically, yes, for sure. And many of them aren't attuned and [don't] understand their energies as well...

...They don't even realize they have energy. They don't have an understanding [that they] have a frequency. So when things begin to change and shift, then yes, it's going to be something that they're not going to understand. They're going to sense certain things, so then they begin to question. Animals don't do that. We already know. So when stuff does begin to change, we understand, and it doesn't affect us as much. Yes, we do feel some physical things, but we understand, so we don't question it. We just relax into it. We allow it to take its course...

...Any human that has an animal around them, like me, or any other pet, or any other animal that they might be around, is helping [with the Great Awakening]. If you connect with that animal, and you're around it all time, you're going to feel the energy change a little differently. Think of it as, they're a bit of a channel for the energy. Kind of a direct connection. So when you get close to your cat, your dog, or any other animal you have, and you have a bond with it, it's going to help with all these changes taking place. It's going to help with the shifts. So I would say, yes, to get connected with your animals. Have a better bond with them, a much closer relationship with them. Then, it'll help you raise your vibration. Sfakiana, female mixed breed dog, age 10

One client asked about the orbs she was seeing in her photos. She wondered if her previous horse, who had already transitioned, had anything to do with them. This horse explained how animals or other energetic beings could create those orbs with their energy.

We push [our aura] out as far as we can. Then we charge the air around us, and if there happen to be little sprites and little other energies that are energized by it, you may capture it on your picture. Bucks Arrow, Thoroughbred gelding, age 11

It's not unusual to observe our pets twitching or vocalizing during nap time. If you're like me, you've probably wondered what they were dreaming about, right?

[I dream of] chasing things! Playing outside, and running, and being on my own. Just being outside by myself and having to find my own food. It's quite interesting, because I do enjoy being taken care of, but it gives me a chance to just run and be free! I do find myself in places that I've never been before in my dreams. There are times that I do get scared in my dreams. Usually it's when I'm with someone I don't like...another animal that I don't care for. Larry, male mixed breed dog, age 5

I subsequently asked if his mom should wake him up when she senses he's having a bad dream.

She can if she wishes, yes. Her touch is always wonderful. Larry, male mixed breed dog, age 5

Cats are intriguing creatures, but they have a reputation for being aloof, not as friendly as dogs. Sometimes, it can even seem like the cat has the upper hand in the relationship. I'm sure all you cat lovers out there have heard the jokes:

"In ancient times cats were worshipped as gods; they have not forgotten this." —Terry Pratchett

"The phrase 'domestic cat' is an oxymoron." —George F. Will

"A dog is a man's best friend. A cat is a cat's best friend."
—Robert J. Vogel

Like horses, cats do tend to have a mind of their own. While it's true that they are much more independent than many pets, a cat with the right personality can be every bit as affectionate as a dog. Here is how one cat described the mystery behind the feline:

By our actions and how we project ourselves in our environment, we may come across as a bit arrogant and not approachable. But when you have the right connection and you have the right understanding of what we're capable of, that's all we want to do, is provide that to you. But yes, we are sometimes not controllable. Once we get into our environment and once we're assigned to where we need to be, we're very protective of it. It becomes our kingdom. And yes, that might come across as a bit strong, but once we're assigned, we know that's where we need to be. That's our mission. We'll do that at all costs. That's why we're here. To be there with that family. Briggite, female domestic shorthair, age 9

Another cat we spoke to called himself the Overseer—he viewed his role as "the manager" of all the other pets in his household. Perhaps not surprisingly, he spoke to us about power.

There's always, in any combination of animals and humans, there's always a balance of power. As we get into trouble, the human, my mother, must provide a bit more power. There are times that I show my dominance, my power, and that is acceptable, as well. Odin, male domestic longhair, age 9

Most felines we've spoken with relish their time as a cat. These two explain why:

It's much more fun being a cat, because we can just lay around, and do what we want, and enjoy ourselves, and find that sunny spot on the floor, and just lay there and relax. Stacy, female domestic shorthair, deceased

I enjoy [being a cat]! It's fun! What's the best way to say it? It's a little ball of energy with a big attitude but a lot of love. Pepper, female domestic shorthair, age 7

If you're a pet parent, you've no doubt had to give your pet some type of medication. You might try disguising it in food or simply tossing it down their throat. Regardless of your technique, it's nearly always an unpleasant ordeal for both the animal and the human.

I know at times I can be a bit of a handful while I'm being given my medication. I don't mean much by it. It's just...I don't think you'd much like it, either, if someone had to do that to you. It's just one of those things. But as soon as it's done, I understand, and I don't think anything bad of [you] for doing it. I know that it's in my best interest. But at the moment, it's not that much fun. I'll try to relax a little bit more so it's a bit easier, and you don't have to worry. I understand. I don't mean to act up at times, but sometimes, it's just a reaction to what's going on. Selah, female domestic shorthair, age 6

While most of the pets we speak with have a favorite treat, they aren't terribly picky about their main meals. Most are just grateful that they have food provided for them (as opposed to having to hunt for it). This cat, though, had a different opinion.

Food-wise, occasionally I would like something a little different. I think it's rather routine eating the same thing over and over again. But I understand. It's just part of being a pet, I guess. Marcy, female domestic shorthair, age 12 (since deceased)

As cat parents ourselves, Will and I have been woken many a night by a cat jumping up on the bed with a toy, ready to play. Frustrated and tired, we exclaim, "Don't you realize it's the middle of the night? It's not play time!" These types of night-time shenanigans make us wonder if cats are really nocturnal animals. Here is how one cat answered that question:

We do tend to play quite hard during the day. Then, we are up during the night. It's not that we're nocturnal, no. We like to sleep at night, too. It's just that when the house is quiet, there's something different. It's just so nice to walk around and see the different energies that come and go that aren't there during the day and experience them differently. So we'll just get up, walk around, see things differently, maybe get in a bit of trouble. But it's just fun when it's quiet like that. Ronin, male domestic shorthair, age 2

This next passage came from a sweet kitty who liked his outdoor time. Occasionally, though, his mom would call for him at night, and he wouldn't come. Other times, he would come home with a few battle wounds. Naturally, she worried. We explained to him how his behavior makes his mom feel and asked if he would consider staying inside the fenced yard. His answer was enlightening—a lesson on choices, fear, and living without regret.

Being outside...it's quite interesting. From the human perspective, you wouldn't think there's much out there, but there's a lot! There are other dogs, other cats, and other animals. And you don't necessarily see them, and you think you're following the same path that you normally take, every day that you go out, and you just wander down that path. Then, one day, there's something there. And it's either, hmm, turn around and go home, or "I want to continue down the path." And I want to continue down the path...

...So I have to make a choice: Do I interact with this other animal and hopefully continue down my path? Sometimes it gets a little rough, but I can handle myself. And yes, I may look a little rough when I come home, but I'm taking care of myself. I know how to mend myself, and yes, be ok. I don't....once that happens, it happens, and it's done, and then I move forward. I don't think about it again, because there's no sense in looking at it and going, "Well, maybe I shouldn't have done that...I shouldn't go down that path anymore...and, maybe I shouldn't do this." Well, then I would just stay at home on my bed, because I'd be too afraid to go outside anymore...

...There's so much more to explore! So it's just enough to make the choice of what you're going to do, and that's what you do! Jasper, male domestic shorthair, age 6

I mentioned to Jasper that I thought humans could learn from his words —not to live in fear but, rather, to courageously take action regardless of possible consequences.

That's correct, yes, and also have the understanding that you can mend yourself. Things will heal [themselves]. And not to worry about it. If you know and you understand your body and yourself, it's all going to take care of itself. Jasper, male domestic shorthair, age 6

As you can see, the pets we speak with offer a never-ending stream of enlightening, engaging, thought-provoking dialogue. They have no hidden agenda, no need to be anything other than who they are. With complete authenticity, our animals meet us where we are, full of grace, forgiveness, and wisdom.

PART II

MAC THE SQUIRREL

The conversation with Mac was important for a couple of reasons. First and foremost, Mac's human mom was concerned about the ethics of keeping a wild animal. She had raised Mac from infancy, when he became separated from his birth mother in the spring of 2019. Once he was old enough, she tried releasing him back into her yard. Sadly, he returned a few days later looking a bit rough. She nursed him back to health and tried releasing him again, but he returned once more, looking even more battered.

At that point, being concerned about his long-term well-being, the family decided to keep Mac in their home. They provided him with appropriate squirrel food, engaging activities, and plenty of love. Nevertheless, his mom still wondered if they had made the right decision. As you'll read below, this arrangement was predestined—Mac and his human mom had made an agreement to intersect in this way. Mac was beyond excited to integrate into a human family, where he could not only receive love but provide it in return.

This session gave Mac's mom the comfort she needed. She no longer had to worry that she was depriving him of his natural "squirrel life." On the contrary, as Mac explains, when humans and wild animals come into relationship (even from afar), it strengthens the interconnectedness of us all![1] Not only was this conversation beneficial to Mac's mom, it also offers us valuable insight regarding squirrels' unique behaviors and thought processes. As with all animals, there is much to be learned from the squirrel population.

～

SPEAKER: Hi, Mac.

MAC: Hello.

SPEAKER: Thank you for coming in! Do you know where you are?

MAC: No.

SPEAKER: You're here speaking to us in a human voice.

MAC: Yes, I hear that! It's different.

SPEAKER: It is. We're going to ask you some questions. Do you mind if we ask you some questions?

MAC: No, it's fine.

SPEAKER: Good! Your mom is here.

MAC: I see that! It's strange because she's here, and I'm here, but I'm also there. It's different. I'm not sure.

SPEAKER: That's true. Your energy is here, your body is there.

MAC: Yes.

SPEAKER: I appreciate you coming in to talk to us. This way, we can understand you a little better. I want to tell you what your mom said first. She says she loves you deep in her soul, she's thankful every day that she's your mom and that you're her Mac, and she's moved to tears when she thinks of you and focuses on your energy in that way. What do you think about that?

MAC: It makes me feel all warm!

SPEAKER: Yes?

MAC: It does! Though she doesn't have to say that. I know that. I sense that. Think of a big bubble that wraps everything up. That's what her energy's like. It's never small. It's always all around everything. It's very comforting, and I love it so much!

SPEAKER: That's nice! Is there anything else you'd like to say to your mom?

MAC: I'm happy that I'm there with you. I thank you for taking care of me and giving me everything I need. It's like I don't have to do anything. Everything's there, right there for me.

SPEAKER: You are in a unique situation in that you're part of a human family, whereas most of the time, squirrels are out in the wild with other squirrels and other animals. Do you understand that?

MAC: I do, yes.

SPEAKER: What do you think about that?

MAC: Well, here's the interesting thing. At some point, you may have thought of this all as a misfortune—that I left my mother, the one that birthed me, and that I didn't grow up like the rest. But you have to understand, this is what you've decided. These are the things you've decided... that you wanted me in your life at this point, and this is how it happens.

SPEAKER: Was this decision made before you incarnated into the body?

MAC: Yes, of course! Before any of us came here, [before] any of us were in any of our bodies, when all of the energy was being lined up. I was part of that energy.

SPEAKER: So you already made this agreement?

MAC: Yes.

SPEAKER: That's beautiful! What was your assignment with this family?

MAC: Love and compassion. But more so, love. And it was unconditional love. Always giving love, no matter the situations, no matter the things that happen. Both of us. I look at things much differently, and I'm always there to find just that little bit of love.

SPEAKER: You definitely are! It sounds like you're a big part of their family, from what I understand.

MAC: Yes.

SPEAKER: That being said, if you all planned this intersection together, then I'm guessing that means you're okay living in the house and don't necessarily want to go live in the wild. Is that correct? Are you okay being in a home for the rest of your life?

MAC: Well, I don't know anything else.

SPEAKER: Right.

MAC: But the interesting thing is, I know what it's like to be outside. I know what it's like to live that life. I've done it before. I know it very well. As fun as that is, there's something magical being with humans. There's a difference. Yes, everything's always provided, but there's—I don't know the word. Many times I see the humans with different pets...cats, dogs, and stuff like that. Those are the ones that are meant to be there.

But when an outside animal is allowed to integrate into the human family, there's a much deeper connection that takes place with your planet and all of the other animals. There's an energy connection that takes place, an understanding. It's like the energy circle all gets connected, all together. There are no missing pieces. Everything is together as one. There's an understanding that takes place between the humans and all animals.

SPEAKER: Wow, that's beautiful and very profound! It sounds to me like even with just one animal and one family, that energy reverberates or ripples out into the whole world. Is that right?

MAC: That's correct, yes. In nature, when an animal even gets close to a human just for a little bit—not necessarily close enough to touch, but their energies are close—that's when that circle is made whole, just for that moment, and you sense it. You understand how it's all ONE, how all of nature, all of your planet, all of the animals, and *you* are connected.

SPEAKER: Wow, that's so nice! Thank you for sharing that. That's good to know so that whenever we do see animals and get close to them, we have a different understanding.

MAC: Yes. When you do, when you're out in the woods, and out somewhere, and all of the animals are around, it's when you're not looking—that's when they come around. Don't try to find them because they've already found you.

SPEAKER: Their energy is much more sensitive. They can sense us before we sense them, for sure.

MAC: Yes.

SPEAKER: That's neat. Thank you for that. Then I guess it's settled; you're okay staying with their family and having a nice, long, healthy life.

MAC: Yes, of course! There are many different things to get into.

SPEAKER: I've heard that! So when you sit in the window, do you see other squirrels outside?

MAC: Yes.

SPEAKER: Do you long for that life, or do you just understand it as different?

MAC: I've lived that life, and I understand it, and someday I'll do that again. But right now, what I think about is, I wish they could experience this.

SPEAKER: Aww!

MAC: I wish they could be in the house, experiencing what I get to experience. The closeness that I have with these humans. It's so different, and so loving, and so caring.

SPEAKER: Beautiful! That's wonderful. That's good to know, because they want your happiness, and they wouldn't want to keep you against your will. So that's wonderful. What do you think about the things that they offer you to play with? They allow you to "bury" nuts, even though they don't have earth to bury it in. But they try to—

MAC: I get to hide them, yes.

SPEAKER: They try to reinforce that for you. Do you like that?

MAC: I like puzzles. I like doing things that I get to think about and try to find things. I try to get into things and try to find things.

SPEAKER: So you enjoy those.

MAC: Yes! I like the challenge.

SPEAKER: Good. You know, squirrels have a reputation for being very smart but also very persistent and kind of ornery.

MAC: We are a wild animal.

SPEAKER: For example, a lot of squirrels like to eat bird feed, so people that like to watch the birds put bird feed out, and they're constantly trying to prevent the squirrels from getting it. But no matter what kind of setup they create, the squirrels always seem to solve the puzzle and get the bird feed. What do you think about that? Why is that?

MAC: It's what we do! If there was something that you enjoyed, and we put it away somewhere, and you really wanted it, wouldn't you do everything trying to find it and get it?

SPEAKER: Sure.

MAC: That's the same way. We enjoy the challenge of something different, but we know what the reward is. We know what's at the other end. The food! And that's what we want. I like the nuts! The nuts are good.

SPEAKER: I guess the difference is that not all animals are quite as persistent or as intelligent.

MAC: Not all. There are some birds that are just as intelligent and persistent as we are. They like to do things, too, and they like the challenge, too. They like to build things to get their food out.

SPEAKER: Do squirrels ever feel offended that humans seem to prefer the birds and want to feed the birds but not the squirrels?

MAC: No, it's just part of nature. Here's the thing. What we like is when you talk to us, and not in a mean way but when you come out and just have a conversation with us. You look at us and tell us that there are others that wish to have that food, as well. We'll mind our business, and we'll have just enough, but we may come back day after day. But we'll leave some.

SPEAKER: That sounds good. We do try to feed the squirrels, putting corncobs and different things in the feeder.

MAC: That's good.

SPEAKER: You told us that you had been squirrels in previous lives. Can you check and see if you've been any other animal or had any other incarnations besides squirrels?

MAC: Most of them have been squirrels. There's one that I see, though, that I was a cat. A small cat. Not a very big cat.

SPEAKER: Was that an indoor or outdoor cat?

MAC: Indoor. I was taken care of by other humans.

SPEAKER: Very neat. I think you live with some cats now, don't you?

MAC: Yes.

SPEAKER: How do you feel about them?

MAC: Sometimes, good; sometimes, bad. I have to watch myself, sometimes. But we get along. Interesting! [Now I] understand! That's why I think I enjoy this so much, because I've already been with humans, so I know what it's like, but I'm just in a different body.

SPEAKER: Right.

MAC: Now, I understand. Interesting!

SPEAKER: Do you think it's enjoyable to be in a home that has other pets, or would you prefer to be an only pet?

MAC: No, it's always fun to have the energy of other animals. It doesn't matter what the animals are, as long as it's other animals. Each one of them has their own separate energy. It can be challenging at times and exciting all at the same time. I would play more, but I think that might be a little difficult.

SPEAKER: To play more?

MAC: Yes.

SPEAKER: With them, you mean? The other cats in the home?

MAC: Yes.

SPEAKER: I see. I understand. I think you're right. Is there anything that your parents need to know to be able to take care of you a little better? Is there anything that needs to change? Anything you need?

MAC: No, other than just more things that challenge me. That's what I like. I like the challenge, the puzzles. Everything is just fine. Here's the interesting thing. It's as if they know exactly what I need and when I need it. It might not be exactly how I want it, but they provide everything at the right time.

SPEAKER: That's beautiful! I'm glad to hear that.

MAC: It's as if they can understand me.

SPEAKER: I think they do. We call that communicating through energy or telepathy, through the mind. Do you sense that you're doing that with them, rather than verbally?

MAC: I don't know. I have not thought [about] that. Maybe. Because I know that there [have] been times that I've thought that I would like something, and shortly thereafter, it's there. Right there with me. That might be.

SPEAKER: Like you said, when we're in the woods, and we sense each other's energy, animals and humans, that's a type of communication. We're saying that we're present. We can use that energy to communicate other things besides just our presence, so perhaps you could practice that with your mom and dad.

MAC: That would be interesting. I think I might try that.

SPEAKER: Very neat. I have a couple of general squirrel questions, if you don't mind.

MAC: Yes.

SPEAKER: Tell me what your viewpoint is—what do you think that squirrels contribute to any community in which they live when they're in the wild? What does the squirrel population contribute?

MAC: That's a very interesting question. I've never thought of it that way, but if you look at what we do, just as much as we like to bury things and then go to retrieve them, we like to stash stuff around. By what we do, by burying a nut or a seed or something, if we can't remember where that is, that nut or seed eventually grows into a new tree or a new bush or something different. So yes, you could call us farmers. We farm stuff! We plant stuff for nature!

SPEAKER: Right!

MAC: We like to keep stuff tidy and clean. All the trees, and all the new branches, and all the old branches. We like to nibble on those and take care of those. We like to clean things.

SPEAKER: Nice! Thank you.

MAC: But in general, we're just part of the bigger connection of all the animals, the big ones and the small ones. It's like a big family.

SPEAKER: That's beautiful! That's so good to hear you say that. What do you think humans can learn by interacting with or observing squirrels?

MAC: To be more resourceful. Yes. If you were to watch us and watch what we do, and how we do things, and when you give us a challenge and how we try to figure it out, it is, as you say, the persistence. It's *that* that we do, and we always come to the end. No matter how long it takes, we always get to the end, where the reward is. It doesn't matter how long it takes, or how many tries, or how much effort goes into it. We just wait it out. We keep doing it until we get it right, and then we have a reward at the end.

SPEAKER: That is good! That's a very good lesson. Humans could definitely learn from that.

MAC: Yes.

SPEAKER: Sometimes, squirrels get into places that humans don't appreciate—for example, our boat. Although it's your nature, you chew things. You sometimes chew things that are damaging to human property, and the humans get kind of aggravated. What's the best way to deter squirrels from getting into places where we don't want them? Is there something we can do that's beneficial for both the squirrel and the human? Is there a natural repellent?

MAC: Just as persistent as we are to go and find some food, we're just as persistent trying to make our nest.

SPEAKER: We've noticed that.

MAC: You say we're damaging things. We don't necessarily look at it like that. It's just something that—it would be as if we were in a tree and a limb was in the way. We'd have to remove that limb. We have to remove certain things to make our nest. But there isn't really anything—no, there really isn't anything that's going to keep us from our mission.

SPEAKER: I see. We don't want to keep you from your mission. We just thought if we could deter you from one area so you would go to another area instead—is there a scent that you don't like or a sign? Something that would say, "Hey, don't go over here, but go over there?"

MAC: Giving an alternative place for us to nest, maybe.

SPEAKER: Your mom suggested that. Could we create some sort of nesting box?

MAC: That might work, yes. You would have to somehow get [us] to be inquisitive enough to go in it. Once we build a nest, and we know it's a secure spot, we'll keep going back to it. No matter how many times it gets taken away, we'll always go back to it.

SPEAKER: We've noticed that with our boat. The other question I wanted to ask is, if a mom is accidentally scared away from the nest, what's the best way to reunite the mom and the babies?

MAC: Just leave it be. Don't touch it. Give it time. We'll be back. We know where our babies are, and we know how to get to them, and we'll do everything to get back to them. Just give it time.

SPEAKER: If a human doesn't realize that the mom is still around and touches the baby, does that prevent the mom from wanting to come back?

Or, after we've touched the baby, can we put it back in the nest? Will the mom still come back, or does the human scent bother it?

MAC: Sometimes, yes. This is interesting because your scent—you call it scent, your smell—it's more the energy. Think of your energy as being what we smell. If we smell or sense that you're angry and upset, and even though you're trying to do the right thing, but yet you're still angry and upset, then yes, we may not come back to that baby. But if you know you're doing the right thing and your energy is caring and loving, even though we don't like the human smell, we understand what you're trying to do, and we will come back.

SPEAKER: Good, thank you for that. That's helpful. What fruits or vegetables are your most favorite?

MAC: It changes from time to time. There are times, especially in the springtime, I like the sweet things. I like the sweet fruits. But then, as it gets warm and it gets near summer, I don't care for those as much. I don't like a lot of green stuff, though it helps, but it's not exactly what I like. Just peanuts, raw peanuts. I like the shells. I like breaking them open and getting inside them. Anything that I like to get into. Stuff I can crack open, and then I can hide them, and then I can go back to them. Popcorn. I like popcorn. Corn. Dried corn. I like that. Especially when it's on the cob. I like to pick at it, and then I fill my cheeks with it, and then I go hide it somewhere.

SPEAKER: How about flowers from the yard? Is the green part more tasty than the flower part? You often flip it upside down and quickly snap the stem off. Is it because it has the taste, or is it in the way?

MAC: Different flowers have different tastes. I don't know which ones they are. But the stem, it's a bit bothersome. It tastes okay, but it's not what I want to eat, so I'll try to get to the softer points and eat those. But the flower itself, they're not that enjoyable. I do like the green, but again, not a lot of it. Sometimes it hurts my stomach, and it's only at certain times that I like that. You have to think of it this way...nuts and grains and stuff like that and small bits of fruit, those are my favorites. And then the green stuff is really helpful for when my stomach has to change a bit. It helps with everything moving through. Yes.

SPEAKER: Good. Digestion.

MAC: Yes.

SPEAKER: Very good. Is there anything you'd like to say to your mom before we close?

MAC: I just want to say thank you! This is exciting! This is fun! Again, it's different. I'm here, there, and everywhere. When you're back home with me, I think we'll be able to talk to each other differently. I think we're going to understand each other differently now that, energy-wise, we've been able to connect like this. I want to tell you that I do love you, and I know how much you love me, and I want to be with you. I want to see how much more fun we're going to have!

SPEAKER: Aww! I think you're going to have a lot of fun, and I think you will understand each other better.

MAC: Yes.

SPEAKER: I just want to say that I'm very, very thankful that you came in to speak with us. I hope to meet you one day.

MAC: That would be fun.

SPEAKER: If I meet you, do you think you'll recognize my energy?

MAC: I think I might, yes.

SPEAKER: Good! Thank you again, Mac. It was such a pleasure talking to you tonight!

MAC: Thank you.

PAARTHURNAX THE BETTA FISH

Paarthurnax's dad actually contacted us because he wanted to speak to the new cat, Siggi, he had recently adopted. Siggi didn't enjoy being cuddled or held and was engaging in some frustrating behaviors. During our consultation, I learned that there was also a pet fish in the household, so we decided to speak to him, as well. I had never spoken to a fish before, so I was excited to hear what he had to say.

Native to Asia, Betta splendens (also called Siamese fighting fish) are enchanting creatures—gorgeous but also complex and sensitive. They recognize their human caretakers and will swim around excitedly when their human approaches. For optimal health, Bettas require a stimulating environment; otherwise, they can become depressed.

The conversation with Paarthurnax didn't disappoint! Interestingly, it was his first time in a physical body, so we spoke a bit about the incarnation process, from his perspective. He also taught us about Betta behavior and why they are infamously known as "fighting fish." In closing, Paarthurnax graced us with some beautiful "fish" wisdom.

PAARTHURNAX: Yes, hello, and I thank you for giving me this experience. I'm quite perplexed by all of it. I'm not quite sure what to make of it, but if you're ok with it, then yes, we can communicate this way.

SPEAKER: Thank you! Your dad would like to know how you like your environment—water temperature, food...

PAARTHURNAX: I don't eat that much, but yes, the food is fine, and the water quality is just fine. He keeps quite a good control of that. I appreciate that. The temperature sometimes is a bit cold, but that's ok, I can adjust. He keeps it at the right temperature, but sometimes, it does drop a bit, but I'm ok with that. He does provide quite a wonderful home for me.

SPEAKER: Do you have a favorite plant in your environment?

PAARTHURNAX: There's one that's almost treelike, and I like to hide behind it, kind of wrap myself into it, but other than that, everything else is adequate.

SPEAKER: Is there anything else you need to make your life better?

PAARTHURNAX: I don't believe so. Everything is provided for. I have a home. I have the...yes, um, I have the proper stuff to survive, yes. The food is just fine; it keeps me healthy.

SPEAKER: What is your assignment with your dad?

PAARTHURNAX: Peace. A sense of peace. When he looks into my environment and sees me swimming there, it takes him into a different place...a comfortable, quiet place...a place of peace.

SPEAKER: Lovely! I understand you have a new kitty in your home. How do you feel about that?

PAARTHURNAX: Yes, I've seen him. I'm not quite sure what to make of him yet. As long as he stays his distance, he should be fine. We can talk to each other at some point, I'm sure. I've tried—he doesn't quite respond yet.

SPEAKER: He's new in the home, so he's still getting used to things.

PAARTHURNAX: Yes, I sense that.

SPEAKER: So tell me about the incarnation process from your perspective, if you will.

PAARTHURNAX: Well, it is quite interesting. So we are all part of one...unity, um, part of one energy. And there's a time...so, there's an understanding that, at a particular time, that we'll break away from that, and we'll be placed into a body, into some form. And in this case, a fish. So it's...we understand that we will be connected to whoever's going to provide for us, or we may be just out in nature by ourselves. We understand that before coming into the body, and I think that for most animals, they understand that they either will be taken care of, or they will be wild, in nature. But in this case, I knew that I was going to be in this body, and I also knew that my dad would be my caretaker, and I wouldn't be out in nature.

SPEAKER: So you knew you'd be with him, specifically?

PAARTHURNAX: We understood that at some point, we would connect.

SPEAKER: You are a Betta fish, also called a fighting fish. Why is that?

PAARTHURNAX: We're very territorial, and we're very fierce when it comes to protecting our space. It's our design, you could say. So if there's another similar type of fish, and even other fish that come into our territory, into our space, around us, our nature is to either fight them off, so they leave, or kill them.

SPEAKER: Wow! So tell me about leaving your birth family after you're born.

PAARTHURNAX: There is no long-lasting tie to, um, you would call it a *parent*. They are just more of a caretaker for the egg that we are in or the body that we inhabit for that amount of time, until we can be out on our own.

SPEAKER: Interesting! So what can we humans learn from fish?

PAARTHURNAX: Hmm, that's an interesting question. Freedom. The freedom to express yourself and live anywhere you wish, no matter the obstacles around you. Being able to move freely, through all things. And also, having a sense of understanding of where you've come from and where you'll go back to. Just knowing that you, through your life, have all the freedom that you wish. You can do whatever you wish to do! Ultimately, in the end, you may be able to do it again and again. Just have the knowing that you're in a place, a special place, to *experience*—the whole time that you're here—no matter the choices you make.

SPEAKER: That's beautiful, thank you! With that in mind, some humans would look at your rather small environment and believe that you really aren't very free, because you are restricted to such a small place.

PAARTHURNAX: That's *your* perspective of our life. We inhabit the space that we're in, and we understand the space that we're in, and we associate that with *our* freedom. This is our movement, and where we can live, and how we can live. Yes, what we don't know is, if there's a place that's bigger. We don't know that. I mean, I guess we could be in a bigger place, but for where we live now, and what we do at this point, that's our freedom, that's our life. I guess I don't quite understand the human's perspective of that. You have all the space, I guess, to do what you wish. But I guess, if someone were looking in on you, where you live, they may say the same thing—that you're restricted by just the small amount of space that you inhabit. But yet, you think it's just enough, and there's enough freedom and enough space to do with what *you* wish.

SPEAKER: Good point! So it's really about perspective.

PAARTHURNAX: Yes

SPEAKER: And being happy with what we have.

PAARTHURNAX: Yes. If my environment were to change, and it were to become bigger, I might not know how to adjust, because I wouldn't know what would be just beyond what I'm used to. But in time, I might get used to it and understand that I have a bit more movement. But then I would become comfortable with that, as well, and I wouldn't look at it as being restrictive.

SPEAKER: Thank you for that wonderful perspective! Is there anything else you'd like to say before we close?

PAARTHURNAX: I just want to say thank you! This has been quite fascinating! It'll be interesting to see, um, yes, to see how [my dad] and I begin to communicate differently now. Maybe we'll understand each other, from my world to your world, and we'll know what each other are thinking.

ROOSTER THE ROOSTER

Our home sits on a little over an acre of land that backs up to a small lake. Because we live in the county, and we don't have a homeowner's association, we are permitted to have "farm" animals. For about ten years, we raised our two fainting goats, Buddy and Lily, as well as a small flock of chickens, thirteen at highest count, mostly hens. At their peak, they were laying about two dozen eggs per week.

Our chickens were always considered our pets. And as such, we entertained ourselves trying to make up cute, creative, or catchy names. Two of our Silkies, Jack and Sparrow, were brother and sister. Checkers was adorable and looked like a black and white checkerboard. At some point, however, it became challenging to not only come up with new names but to try to remember them all—after all, it was like having thirteen children! Plus, as the older birds passed, new chicks were born—it became untenable. So we stopped.

Our goats have transitioned, and we are now down to a single rooster... whom we simply call, Rooster. The poor thing has had a bit of a rough life, and as a youngster, never really wanted to bond with us (or his fellow chickens, for that matter). Now that he's all alone, we've become much closer. While Buddy and Lily were alive, he had fun hanging out with them. They provided him with companionship and a bit of protection. After they passed, however, Rooster had an unfortunate run in with a neighbor's dog who had gotten loose. Luckily, Rooster was not injured, but he was badly shaken up. He no longer felt safe in his coop and has since taken up residence on a rocking chair on our front porch. (He's startled quite a few Amazon delivery drivers!)

Our conversation reassured us that although he is alone, with no chickens to protect, we needn't worry—he is doing just fine. He actually admitted to kind of enjoying his newfound freedom!

～

ROOSTER: Hello!

SPEAKER: Hi! Thank you for speaking with us. Roosters are known for their crow. Tell me, what are you communicating through your crow?

ROOSTER: It's more of just, um, either responding to or calling out to the other chickens that are in this area. I hear them. They're in the distance, and we talk to each other that way. We're communicating. We let each other know that everything's ok in our area. And then, they respond by the same. It's kind of a warning. If there's something in the area that might be threatening to us, we call out. We also listen for the call from others.

SPEAKER: Oh, wonderful! What about your morning crows?

ROOSTER: It's just to let all the others that are around know that I'm awake and ready to respond.

SPEAKER: Some people aren't too thrilled about loud crows in the morning. What would you like to tell them?

ROOSTER: I'm sorry, but that's how it is! We—all chickens—once we awake for the morning, that's what we do. We just let everyone know that we are awake and are ready to respond. We're very protective. We respond to all things that may be dangerous to us. We sense other animals in the area...other birds that are flying around that might harm us. We just call out and let everyone know, in the area, that they're around.

SPEAKER: What types of predators do you look out for? Hawks, bald eagles?

ROOSTER: Yes, those are some, but there are others that are on your property that come back and forth. There are some small dogs, there are also a few cats that roam around outside. There are also some raccoons that come to visit every so often. They're not very friendly. But other than that, it's pretty quiet.

SPEAKER: Is the rooster's role primarily to protect a flock of chickens?

ROOSTER: Yes, it's to look out over chickens, yes.

SPEAKER: So how do roosters do when alone?

ROOSTER: Sometimes, it's a bit lonely since we like to have others around—those are the ones we'd be protecting—but I've been here by myself for quite a while. I haven't had any other chickens to protect. So it's a bit different. Now it's just me, and I'm ok with that. I know the property, and I know where I can and can't go. And now that I can go everywhere, it's a bit more exciting, because I can find different things to eat. You've taken great care of me, and I appreciate that. And I know that you'll watch out over me up until the day I have to leave.

SPEAKER: I'm so sorry that you have to be by yourself, but I'm glad you are doing ok! Tell me, do you enjoy being a rooster?

ROOSTER: For the most part. It has its ups and downs. I enjoy being the one that protects. The one that watches out over.

SPEAKER: Is there anything you dislike about being a rooster?

ROOSTER: Similar things...having to watch out over many chickens. It's a lot easier when you're having to watch out over yourself, but if you have a whole flock to watch over, it's a bit difficult. Sometimes, you lose track of them, and it becomes a bit stressful.

SPEAKER: Yes, I can imagine! What do humans need to know about roosters?

ROOSTER: I think that there's a misunderstanding that we're dangerous, we're not easily tamed, that we'll get in trouble. But that's with any animal. You have to be with them right from the beginning...make that connection, that bond. We haven't bonded very well. I was a bit nervous around everyone, so I never really bonded or connected to you.

SPEAKER: That's true, you were a little stand-offish. But we've felt a bit guilty that you're by yourself now that the goats have passed, so we've tried to make an extra effort to bond with you. Have you noticed that?

ROOSTER: Yes, and that's why I've been coming around. It may not be as strong of a bond, but yes, that's why I've been coming around.

SPEAKER: It's quite endearing when you come up on the back porch in the morning and call to us. Are you asking for food?

ROOSTER: Not always, I'm just letting you know that I'm there and... waking you up.

SPEAKER: Well, thank you for that. What was your assignment with our family?

ROOSTER: Patience, to be patient with me. I was a bit of a struggle at first. I didn't get along with many of the other chickens either, so it was a bit difficult. But I think things have been getting better.

SPEAKER: What was your relationship with the goats, Buddy and Lily?

ROOSTER: Hmm, Lily was a bit rambunctious, and she would push us aside. I think that was just her way of showing that she was kind of the "big" person. But Buddy, he was more comfortable. He would like it when we would lay up against him...be on him....kind of give him a back scratch. It was a comfortable relationship. He was more easy-going.

SPEAKER: Yes, you are exactly right! Thank you for speaking with us today. Is there anything else you'd like to share before we close?

ROOSTER: Thank you for everything you've done. You've provided well for me, and I'll continue to provide for you....the entertainment I think you're looking for.

15

MYRTLE THE TORTOISE

Myrtle's dad was devastated by the untimely loss of his beloved pet. In tortoise years, she was only a young adult. Myrtle and her dad had grown up together, but her passing occurred while he was working out of town. Sadly, he had not been able to say goodbye. During our conversation, Myrtle was able to provide her dad with the comfort of knowing that all was well—she was happy in the afterlife. In fact, she was busy assisting other animals who were getting ready to incarnate for the first time! As we chatted, Myrtle was able to share a bit more about how the incarnation process works, explain the differences between tortoises and turtles, and offer some profound wisdom for humanity.

MYRTLE: I am present

SPEAKER: Thank you very much, Myrtle, for being present with us! Your dad was very sad by your loss. Can you tell us where you are now, please?

MYRTLE: Yes, the....you have to understand that when any animal transitions, the body is no longer needed. So just the essence, the energy....it's hard to explain what it looks like from the human side. Just think of a big ball of energy that leaves and then gets reunited with *everything*...all the energy, all the energies of everything, all connected together. And it becomes one big, beautiful place. There are all the animals, all the humans...*everything*! Everything you can imagine, all together at once. But if you were to look at it, it would just be a big glow, like a big mass of white light. But inside that white light, there's everything. Everything that exists! So that's where I am. So yes, it's a comfortable place. But, there's always something to do...ready to go into another body, help with other energies that are getting ready to go into another body....so, it's a bit busy!

SPEAKER: That sounds fun! It sounds like you're happy.

MYRTLE: Yes!

SPEAKER: So you have not come into another body yet?

MYRTLE: No

SPEAKER: And when you say, *"help with others coming into a body,"* how do you help? What do you do?

MYRTLE: If they haven't been, we sometimes...when they're getting ready, we're just there to guide them, help them. They may not understand exactly what's going to take place. But we're there to help them and have them understand what's going to take place and that one moment they're here, and the next moment, they're in something physical. They're part of a different body.

SPEAKER: Is that kind of an abrupt change for them? Is it startling at first?

MYRTLE: Yes, but only for a very small amount of time, because it is....when you're body-less, and you have no place or space, and then you enter into something that you're confined to, it is a bit difficult, yes.

SPEAKER: I bet! Thank you for that explanation. So, what was your assignment with your dad?

MYRTLE: Patience. The understanding of patience. You see, we're not the fastest at anything, whether that's growing or doing something. We require patience to do everything that we do. So it was to teach him to just slow down, and enjoy, and just wait for those moments.

SPEAKER: I don't know if you can speak for all of the turtles and tortoises, but do you think that is a message that you all have for humanity? To learn patience? Or, is there a greater message for us?

MYRTLE: I would say that, yes, patience. But it is understanding just to take your time. There's no need to rush. There's no need to go fast, because when you go fast, you miss a lot. There's a lot that's happening when you just slow yourself down...just enough to see what's going on. You'll actually *see* more. You'll *understand* more. You'll *feel* more. Though, it's just to slow down and understand that even though you feel that your life is going by quickly, it's really not, and just to take the time to understand what's there, in front of you...at every moment, at every second.

SPEAKER: Thank you, that's a great message! I've never spoken to a turtle or tortoise. What do you see as the difference between turtles and tortoises?

MYRTLE: One is our size. But we're very similar. Tortoises enjoy space. We enjoy being on the land. There are some turtles, I think, that enjoy their time in the water, or they like to be where it's wet. They enjoy the wet areas. But overall, we're very similar. It's just that we enjoy each moment, and we don't have anywhere we need to be. We just enjoy each moment and everything that's provided for us. Turtles, they enjoy the same, but they like to do a bit more exploring. They like to go different places. So they might not stay in an area very long. They like to go and travel.

SPEAKER: I could understand that. I see them wandering around a lot... through the yard, across roads, and all sorts of places. When you were with your dad, in the tortoise body, you had many dog-siblings that lived with you. How did you enjoy that experience?

MYRTLE: That was interesting. There was a particular energy they had. It was quite playful but yet, very strong, like they were there to watch over everything, like they were protecting me and watching out. Not only for me but everything on the property. Overall, they didn't bother me much. They weren't around a lot with me, no.

SPEAKER: When you passed, it was rather sudden and unexpected. Because of that, it was a little traumatic. Is there anything you'd like to say about that experience?

MYRTLE: You have to understand, that, though to you it may have seemed tragic and quick, and it was unfortunate, when we enter into a body, we know all the way to the end...we understand what's going to happen. It isn't for us to tell you what's going to happen, even if we could. It's just to enjoy every moment with you. So at that point, I knew this was going to be the time, because I was needed somewhere else. All the circumstances were there to make that happen. We understand that, but what you have to know is that even though I'm no longer there, I'm still connected to you. I'm still there, connected through your energy. There's always going to be that connection. And that's with any pet that transitions. There's always just a little bit of energy that stays with the human, after [we] transition.

SPEAKER: Sometimes we can sense that, and sometimes we don't.

MYRTLE: Yes, that's correct.

SPEAKER: Do you have any other messages for humanity?

MYRTLE: Just enjoy the time that you have with us! Sometimes, when we're with you for so long, you sometimes forget about us or take us for granted...that we'll always be there. Just remember, we're always with you, whether you're physically with us or you're separated from us. You can always just send us your love. You can energetically just think about us, and we'll understand, and we'll feel that, and we'll respond back to you. Just take each moment and enjoy it!

16

SASA THE BOMB-SNIFFING DOG

Sasa is a nine-year-old, female, black Labrador retriever. Sasa's dad requested a session with us primarily because Sasa had experienced a "panic attack" one day while walking up the stairs in his home. She was terrified and refused to move. Although Sasa had never really liked stairs, this incident was different…it seemed to have come out of nowhere. Of course, Sasa's dad was quite concerned—he certainly didn't want to sell his home, but he also didn't want to carry his big girl up and down the stairs each day.

During the consultation, we spoke about Sasa's behavior and at first, assumed there was some sort of physical issue. After all, she was getting older, and arthritis is a common condition amongst elderly Labs. Interestingly, Sasa's dad also shared that she had been a working dog—a bomb sniffing canine in the United States Army—and had been forced into an early retirement due to unexplained stress. When he adopted her, however, he had not been given any details about what types of stress-related behaviors she was exhibiting or what, specifically, prompted her "discharge." I was eager to speak to Sasa, not only to learn about her time with the Army but to ascertain whether she was still experiencing post-traumatic stress symptoms, and if so, how we could help.

Curiously, we still weren't making the connection between Sasa's role in the Army and the stair-climbing issue, but what we discovered during this conversation was astonishing! Not only did Sasa explain the origin of the issue, she told us exactly how to help her overcome the problem. She also gave us incredible insight about the life of a military working dog and shared why she might never be ready to fully "retire!"

SPEAKER: You have always been what we call a working dog. You have important jobs to do.

SASA: Yes.

SPEAKER: The first one, you were in the Army, sniffing for bombs. Tell me about that.

SASA: I don't know what you'd like to know. It's an interesting thing. It's not what I expected to do. You see, for most of my life, I thought I was going to be just another dog with a family somewhere, waiting to this point when I'm with my father and just relaxing with him. But as with life, things happen. Someone came and got me, I guess because I was a quiet dog. I wasn't overly loud, like a lot of them, and I just sat patiently. They came and got me.

From there, it was quite interesting. I was doing a lot of fun things! They played with me quite a bit and taught me how to do all kinds of stuff. Stuff that I like to do. I like to search for stuff. I like to smell for stuff. So that's what they did; they showed me how to do that even more. I really didn't think much about it. It was just that part of my life—a lot of neat and interesting people that I met; they always took care of me. They always played with me. Sometimes, even to the point where we'd get rough with each other, because it was like I was part of them, and they were part of me. We were all one big pack!

SPEAKER: With other dogs?

SASA: No.

SPEAKER: Just with the humans?

SASA: With my humans that took care of me, yes. It was like we were one big pack. They would play with me, and I'd play with them, and then we'd have to go do something. I was important for that moment. They'd give me an opportunity to do something, and then—I don't know, I guess just doing what I did, they would reward me and play with me even more.

SPEAKER: That's fascinating! I didn't know if you had hung out with the other dogs, if there were other dogs that did the same thing.

SASA: There were several, but we kept our distance from one another. Occasionally, we would meet, but we were usually separated.

SPEAKER: Was there one primary companion that you stuck with most of the time, or did you work with several different humans?

SASA: Well, there was one human that was my main caregiver. But at times, yes, he would let me go with others, and they would watch over me and allow me to do certain things.

SPEAKER: I see. Are you saying, then, that when you were cleaved off from Source and came into this body, you didn't know that you were going to have this job?

SASA: No.

SPEAKER: That's interesting.

SASA: Yes, this was quite unexpected. So yes, I don't know. It's not what I planned. If you could see—coming in, yes, I knew that I was going to be by myself for a while, and I knew that I'd be with other dogs, and at some point I knew that a human was going to come and get me. But I knew it wasn't my father, and I knew it wasn't him who was going to take me home, and that's where I was going to be. It was going to be a different human.

SPEAKER: Until the time that you could meet up with your dad.

SASA: Yes. I knew that another human was going to take care of me for quite a while, but I didn't know what I was going to be doing. So yes, to an extent, I knew that there was going to be another human. I didn't know I was going to have such an important role.

SPEAKER: Neat! Yes, you were very important over there. You said that you would get rewarded when you would do this mission.

SASA: Yes.

SPEAKER: Do you understand that one of the reasons that you got rewarded so nicely was because it was a pretty dangerous mission? Were you aware of that?

SASA: No. I like to dig, I like to sniff, I like to hunt things down, and they would teach me how to do that better. So that's what I did! When I smelled something, and I knew that that was something I had to let my human know, that's when they would reward me.

SPEAKER: Wonderful! So when you found this *something*, what behavior did you do? How did you alert your human?

SASA: Most of the time I would just sit, and I would stare. I wouldn't move. Just look at it. Then they would come over, and then they would slowly pull me away, and then we'd play a bit.

SPEAKER: Nice. Do you know what it was you were searching for?

SASA: I don't know. I just know the smell. Yes, I know the smell. I know what that smell is. Yes.

SPEAKER: The thing that you were searching for, we call it a bomb. It can blow up and explode. Do you remember hearing some loud noises?

SASA: Yes, I understand that now. Yes! Yes, now I understand! As we were playing, then there would be other humans that would come in to do something, and then they would put me in my kennel in the back of the vehicle, and then there'd be a loud noise. It would kind of shake the vehicle.

SPEAKER: So that's what was happening. How would you feel when that noise would happen? Was it scary, or were you okay with it?

SASA: At first it was scary, but then you got used to it. You realized that —yes, I would smell something, I'd sit, we'd play, and then a bit later, that noise would happen.

SPEAKER: I see. What was happening was they were detonating or setting off that bomb that you found for them, so that other humans or animals would not get hurt. That was a very important job!

SASA: Yes!

SPEAKER: We're proud of you for doing that. Your dad is very proud of you, too.

SASA: Thank you!

SPEAKER: I have a question, then. Because of that, do you think that you have some anxiety or nervousness because of that history as a bomb-sniffing dog? Do you tend to be nervous now about anything?

SASA: Sometimes.

SPEAKER: What are you nervous about?

SASA: Noises, sometimes. Not often. It's more just random different things. I don't know if it's [that] I get nervous, but I want to look for it. I want to find it. If I hear a noise, I have to look, and I have to find it to make sure everything's okay.

SPEAKER: Part of your role as a protector.

SASA: Yes.

SPEAKER: What about stairs? Your dad tells me that you get kind of upset about stairs. What's going on with that behavior?

SASA: Some of it is I'm a bit older now, and it's a bit uncomfortable at times. But—yes. Well, I know—you have to understand, to get in my kennel after we'd get done playing, and after I find the *thing*, and we play, I have to go up...it's not really stairs. It was more like...I don't know. It wasn't like I jumped into the vehicle.

SPEAKER: But you had at least a step?

SASA: It was like this long thing I had to walk up.

SPEAKER: A ramp? Like a long, flat—something long and flat that led from the ground up into your—

SASA: Yes, yes! Sometimes, I didn't make it all the way in there before that loud sound.

SPEAKER: Oh! So you paired, in your mind, a loud sound with walking up the ramp.

SASA: Going up, yes.

SPEAKER: Fascinating!

SASA: Yes, because I knew that once I was in my kennel, I was safe, and I knew that nothing was going to happen. Even with the sound.

SPEAKER: But sometimes, you weren't already in your kennel safely.

SASA: Right.

SPEAKER: I see. Do you think that has something to do, now, with going upstairs? Are you still associating it with that?

SASA: Some of it, yes, because I'm afraid that I'm not going to make it all the way to the top before something happens.

SPEAKER: I see. What about going down? Is it the same feeling when you're going down the stairs?

SASA: That's different. It just might be me not being comfortable going down the stairs.

SPEAKER: While we're talking about that, let's do a body scan. Can you do a body scan and let me know how you're feeling in your body? Are there any issues we need to be aware of?

SASA: While everything seems to be fine, there's some—not always, but some soreness in my back legs. With my stomach, there's a bit of tenderness with that. And then there's...it's hard to describe. It feels like—and this isn't all the time either, but it feels like there's something pushing on my head.

SPEAKER: Interesting. Let's focus on that. Where does that feel like it's coming from, this pressure on your head?

SASA: It's kind of in the middle, and it's like it's pushing out.

SPEAKER: And it only happens, sometimes?

SASA: Yes. Not always.

SPEAKER: When do you think it normally happens? In the morning or in the evening, or when you're playing, or when you're resting...?

SASA: Sometimes, when I get up from a rest and I'm trying to get up, it hurts a little bit. It feels like everything wants to push out.

SPEAKER: I see.

SASA: And then when there's a lot of excitement, that's another time.

SPEAKER: Do you notice any other symptoms or issues when that pain happens? For example, does it make your eyes blurry or your ears ring?

SASA: I know I want to scratch my ears.

SPEAKER: So you think it might have something to do with your ears?

SASA: No, it's not—no. I don't think so.

SPEAKER: You're doing a fantastic job, Sasa. I really appreciate it! What I'd like for you to do is to focus on your head and see if you see any light. Do you see anything lighting up in your head, showing you where the pain might be coming from or maybe a growth or something that doesn't belong there?

SASA: No.

SPEAKER: Okay. Do you think that it needs to be looked at by your doctor?

SASA: At the moment I don't think so. I mean, it's there for a moment, it's uncomfortable, and I kind of want to shake my head and get it out, and then as I start doing something, it does go away. I don't know if it's anything—when I was telling you that I didn't make it back to my kennel and then I'd hear the noise, that's kind of what it felt like when the noise would happen. It was very uncomfortable.

SPEAKER: I wonder if it caused a concussion. You may not know that word, but your dad will know. Or maybe the ringing in the ear, so that maybe there's some balance issues or something like that. Your dad can keep an eye on you, if that's okay.

SASA: Yes, that's what I would like. That's the one thing that my humans would tell me. I would tell them when anything was wrong, and they would have me looked at. I know how to do that.

SPEAKER: Excellent! That's beautiful. How did you tell them when there was something wrong?

SASA: Sometimes, I'd whimper. I'd sit next to them, and I'd whimper. Then, sometimes, I could take my paw and...not hold it...when my ear would hurt, I would put my paw there, and I'd scratch it and I'd look at my owner.

SPEAKER: Excellent! Your dad can hear this, so he'll know now to pay extra attention to your behaviors. That's beautiful, thank you. Now, you said your back legs are a little stiff and sore. Do you think that is the problem with going downstairs?

SASA: It may be. It's right in my back and where my legs are. It's not always, but yes.

SPEAKER: We'll be mindful of that and maybe help you get up and down the stairs. But I am kind of concerned about this going up the stairs, and with the anxiety, because your dad tells me that you had what we call a panic attack, and I guess you froze, or you weren't able to go up the stairs at all, or you just really freaked out.

SASA: Yes.

SPEAKER: Can you remember when that happened? Can you look back at that event?

SASA: Yes, I remember.

SPEAKER: What was going on when that happened?

SASA: I wasn't sure if I was going to make it to the top before another loud noise would happen, and I wanted to be safe. I just got worried and had to stop, because I didn't know what to do.

SPEAKER: I understand, and we're so sorry that you have that problem and that you had to have that experience in the first place. We're very sorry about that. Is there anything that your dad can do to make you more comfortable? What can we do to help you so that you don't have this anxiety going upstairs?

SASA: I don't know. But when my humans would show me how to do something, [when] they wanted me to do a certain thing, they wouldn't do everything at once. They would just get me to do something, and then they would reward me, and then sit with me, and play with me, and talk to me. And then we'd go do something else, and then we'd come back to that, and they would do a little bit more.

SPEAKER: Beautiful. So maybe he can reward you and help start to train you, or re-train you, to go back upstairs?

SASA: Yes.

SPEAKER: Excellent! That's good advice.

SASA: Just watch me, because I don't want to do that again.

SPEAKER: Sure! It's not comfortable, no. Good! I think we're making great progress, Sasa. Thank you for your help! I really appreciate that. I have another line of questions for you, and this is sort of in general to a lot of dogs. Do dogs in general—and I don't know if you feel that you can speak for many dogs—but do you think dogs enjoy having a job or a mission, like you did when you were a bomb sniffing dog? Do dogs like to work like that?

SASA: That's a good question. I know that that isn't what I expected for my life. I knew that I was going to be with a human, and I knew that I was going to do something, but I didn't know what. But now that I've done it, I enjoyed it, yes. I don't know—I can't say for the other dogs, but I know that I enjoyed every minute of it. It was exciting! Even though it was difficult at times, learning all the new stuff, I enjoyed it. I wanted to do it more, and I wanted to help my other humans.

SPEAKER: Neat! Good. Now, you're also trained as a therapeutic dog, a therapy dog, a dog that goes different places to help for different things. For example, I think for a while you went to the police department, and you were helping in different situations where maybe you brought comfort to a child or maybe somebody who's sick, right?

SASA: Yes.

SPEAKER: Do you enjoy that?

SASA: Yes, I do! I do!

SPEAKER: You had to be trained for that mission.

SASA: Yes.

SPEAKER: That's what I mean when I say "working," where dogs are trained to go on certain missions like that to help people.

SASA: Yes. If my human wants me to help them in any way, that's what I'm there for.

SPEAKER: That's amazing!

SASA: I wouldn't want to do anything else. If my human wanted me to do something, and they showed me how to do it, that's what I'd want to do.

SPEAKER: When you take on that role, your dad says he puts a service vest on you, and all of a sudden you change. You're, I guess, excited? Tell me about that.

SASA: Yes, it makes me feel like I did with my other humans again, because that was the same thing. They'd put something around me, and I felt very important at that time. And I knew that at that point, I had to do something. I've got to do what they showed me to do. That's when I would get rewarded. So yes, when my father puts that vest on me, I feel like I'm doing what I was meant to do.

SPEAKER: That's wonderful! That's beautiful. Your dad wanted me to ask you—he was thinking you've done so much work throughout your life that perhaps you want to do what we call *retirement*, where you just get to not work anymore and just relax, and play, and have fun.

SASA: I get enough playing. I get enough relaxing. If there are times that he wishes for me to be with him and to do certain things, I'm fine with that.

SPEAKER: Good!

SASA: I enjoy being around people! That's what I want to do.

SPEAKER: Excellent! That's beautiful. I'm so excited to hear that. It sounds like you're going to have a long life helping others. That's wonderful!

SASA: I want to do that, yes!

SPEAKER: Good! Is there anything else that you can think of that is reminding you of any stress or anxiety that you had in the past? Is there anything that needs to change in your environment, or with your family, or in your home that reminds you of any of that anxiety?

SASA: My father is doing a wonderful job! I guess, teach me how to be more calm in my home. There are a lot of noises, but I'm understanding the difference now between what it used to be, that kind of noise, to what these noises are. Yes, they still alert me, and I want to find them, but it's not as scary.

SPEAKER: Wonderful!

SASA: But what's interesting—I know I'm going to understand my father better now, and I understand what he wants of me. I'm looking forward to this! Yes, I do enjoy, as you say, working. I don't look at it that way. It's just another way for me to have fun and be with people.

Sasa's dad shared the following information with us after the session. His amazing story provides inspiring evidence that our pets are divinely guided to us—there are no coincidences!

"When I applied to adopt a military working dog, I wanted a German shepherd. I wanted nothing else. I waited on a waiting list for almost two years and finally said, 'Ok, what do you have available?' They sent me a bunch of pictures of Labs, and I sort of scrolled through them with this half-hearted, 'I guess if I have no choice, I'll get a Lab.' And [then] I saw

Sasa's picture, and my whole heart changed, and it was almost like, 'Oh my God! I found the dog that I lost and didn't even know I lost her!' And when I picked her up at the airport, we instantly bonded. I think we each fight over who takes care of whom. I always tell her she treats me like I am her puppy, and I try to remind her she is my puppy!"

17

A PAST LIFE HEALING FOR MAXIMUS

Maximus is a six-year-old male cockapoo who had recently experienced two seizures. In both cases, the seizures had been induced by a high-pitched noise. Naturally, Maximus's mom was extremely concerned about his well-being. In addition, Maximus barked...a lot. In fact, much to his mom's frustration, Maximus's barking provoked his biological sister, Isabella, to start barking, as well.

We spoke to both Maximus and Isabella during this session. While it's always enjoyable to talk to multiple pets in a household, the conversation with Maximus, specifically, was incredible for another, more dramatic reason. Although I have a fairly thorough understanding of reincarnation and past lives, it wasn't until this conversation with Maximus that I realized that animals could actually be affected by past life trauma, similar to the humans I work with in my quantum healing practice. I'm not sure why I was surprised; perhaps simply because I hadn't encountered it yet. Needless to say, this was a very special session that paved the way for even deeper levels of healing among the animals we were called to work with.

Inserted within the transcript below, I've provided commentary (in italics) designed to shed light on my thought process as I navigated my way through this unique session.

~

MAXIMUS: Hello?

SPEAKER: Hi, Maximus!

MAXIMUS: Hello.

SPEAKER: How are you doing?

MAXIMUS: Fine.

SPEAKER: You look a little confused.

MAXIMUS: Yes.

SPEAKER: You're here in a new place, speaking to us in a human voice so that we can understand you better.

MAXIMUS: I hear that, yes. Yes. Interesting.

SPEAKER: It is interesting.

MAXIMUS: Okay. I'm assuming—yes, I'm assuming my mom is here somewhere. Yes, I feel her now. Yes.

SPEAKER: She is here. Would you like to say hello?

MAXIMUS: Yes, yes, yes! Hello, Mom! I want to say I'm not sure what I'm doing, but you're here, so I'm okay. And I think everything'll be fine, but I want to say that I appreciate everything you've done. Your voice and your touch—that's the most comforting to me. When I'm nervous, and when I'm excited, and when I feel a bit anxious, I just like to hear your voice, and it makes me feel so comfortable. Yes! But I'll trust that everything'll be fine, and I'll be okay.

SPEAKER: You will be. You'll be fine! We did want to ask a few questions, if that's okay.

MAXIMUS: That's fine.

SPEAKER: Speaking of nervousness, do you tend to be anxious or nervous a lot?

MAXIMUS: Sometimes I don't show it, but there's quite a bit of times that things...there are things I think about, and it's not that I don't like where I'm going or [what I'm] doing, but there's something...it's difficult to express. When we go out, and when we go places, I'm not sure where we're going. I know Mom tells us that we're going to go somewhere, and we're going to do something, but I'm just a bit nervous that I'm not sure exactly where we're going. I like to know *exactly*. But I understand, sometimes that's not always possible. And different people make me a bit cautious. Yes.

SPEAKER: So what would be helpful? Would you prefer that your mom be more specific when she tells you where you're going?

MAXIMUS: Well, yes, being more specific would help, I think. She does a lot for me, and she always is next to me, and is telling me stuff, but it's just that—well, when you—see, right now I'm nervous, and I don't have my words.

SPEAKER: It's okay. You can relax. Everybody here loves you! Can you sense our love for you?

MAXIMUS: I do, I do!

SPEAKER: Good!

MAXIMUS: Everything is exciting and new, and I want to explore, but also I'm just a bit afraid. Not afraid that I'm going to do something wrong or something's going to happen. It's just...I don't know what's out there.

SPEAKER: Afraid of the unknown.

MAXIMUS: Yes. And even though Mom tells me, "We're going to go to the park, and we're going to go do things," I still don't know. I know we're going to the park, but there's still things I don't know, and it makes me a bit nervous.

SPEAKER: I understand. Humans have that problem as well, sometimes. What can your mom do to help you with that? Is there anything that she can do, or is that just your personality?

MAXIMUS: Yes, I think some is my personality. Just more comfort. I know she gives me enough already, but—I know, sometimes, I'm a big baby. I just need to be comforted. Yes.

SPEAKER: I see. What about high-pitched noises? Apparently you've had what we call a seizure. You've had two seizures because of high-pitched noises. What is it that bothers your ears? Can you check in with your body and let us know what's going on there?

MAXIMUS: This is hard to describe. When that happens—it's like when I don't know I'm going somewhere, and I don't know what's going to happen. I get nervous, and I want to be close to Mom, and sometimes, I get a little shaky about things. It's kind of like that. I get eased into it, and Mom is there with me the whole time. But when that happens with the noise...I don't know, and it startles me, and inside it's like everything goes blank. I can't tell you exactly, but it's like when Mom turns the lights on in the room. Everything goes bright and blank, and I don't remember.

SPEAKER: So are you saying even bright lights are causing you to go into that state?

MAXIMUS: No.

SPEAKER: It's just an example.

MAXIMUS: That's the example. When that loud noise happens, it's like turning on the lights in the room. It gets really bright, and then I don't remember.

SPEAKER: So it's causing your mind and your body to go into a state of extreme anxiety, I guess, to the point where you sort of shut it off?

MAXIMUS: Yes, I think so. I just know that…I'm trying to remember some of the times. I hear the noise, and then it gets really bright, and then I forget, and then I don't know from that point.

SPEAKER: That would be a description of a seizure. Is the body twitching when that happens? So your body's twitching? You remember that?

MAXIMUS: Yes. Yes, but I don't remember anything. I don't really see anything. When I first hear it, I understand the feeling. It's like not knowing where I'm going. But then it happens so fast, I don't remember anything else.

SPEAKER: I understand. So your body's automatically reacting to that.

MAXIMUS: Yes. I'm trying to… [pause, whimpering] Yes. Okay, yes.

At this point, Maximus made the connection that his seizures were related to something that happened in his previous lives. As he revisits those memories, he starts to whimper. Because I don't know what he is "seeing," I ask several follow up questions to try to pinpoint the original source of the issue.

SPEAKER: What happened that made you sad? What did you recognize?

MAXIMUS: Yes. This is from something before I was in this body. This is something that took place before I was in this body. This is just a way of protecting myself.

SPEAKER: Tell us about that life, please. What was going on that caused that?

MAXIMUS: I see it. Yes. In that life—it's interesting, because I see different lives where similar things happen. And I was different animals. I wasn't always a dog.

SPEAKER: So this happened multiple times?

MAXIMUS: Yes.

SPEAKER: What types of animals were you?

MAXIMUS: One looks to be a horse. And then...yes, I was a dog. And a bear, I guess. I don't understand what I'm seeing. For each time, there was a loud sound with a bright flash, and that's where it ends.

SPEAKER: So tell me, do you think this was lightning coming from the sky that caused your death?

MAXIMUS: No. No, it was not. No. This was something that was...

SPEAKER: And was it a noise and a light?

MAXIMUS: Yes. And there were other humans there.

SPEAKER: And each time, did it cause your death? Or was it just a startling event?

MAXIMUS: No, that's where it ends, and then I'm into the next body.

SPEAKER: Wow, okay.

MAXIMUS: Yes. So each time that happens, then I move into the next body, and then that happens [again], and I move into the next body.

SPEAKER: I guess I'm trying to find out if that was *causing* the death of your physical body, or is that just a phenomenon that happens when you transition from this—

MAXIMUS: No, that's not it. No, that's definitely not it.

SPEAKER: It was a scary thing that happened. A frightening—

MAXIMUS: But each time there's a human there. Each time there's a human, and then it ends. Just a loud sound, and a flash of light, and then it ends. And then I'm into the next body.

SPEAKER: But you're unable to tune in to find out what was happening right before that flash of light? Are you saying that perhaps the human did something that caused your death?

MAXIMUS: It may be, because there's something with them that does that, and I don't know what that is.

SPEAKER: And it's a bear, a horse, and a dog?

MAXIMUS: Yes. Horse first, then dog, and then bear. Yes.

SPEAKER: Were you a wild animal or were you in a home as a dog, for example?

MAXIMUS: I was not in a house like I am now, no. I was outside, but I was taken care of by humans. I don't understand what I'm seeing.

SPEAKER: I wonder if it was like a bomb of some sort.

MAXIMUS: I don't know.

SPEAKER: Well, at any rate, I appreciate you looking into that, because I know that's not a comfortable thing to watch.

MAXIMUS: No.

All of a sudden it occurred to me that those three animals had been shot. Each situation may have been different, however. For example, perhaps the bear was shot because he was a threat to the human or was being hunted. The horse may have been shot as he was ridden into battle. There was not enough time—and really no need—to investigate the specifics of those deaths, particularly since it was upsetting to Maximus. That being said, Maximus provided a clue later in the conversation by stating that in those lives, he was his humans' protector, just as he is in this life.

In a flash of inspiration, I decided to attempt to facilitate the healing of those residual past-life traumas. Although I have plenty of experience working with past life issues in humans, through hypnosis, I had never encountered this situation in an animal session. But, I reasoned, if it could provide relief for Maximus and comfort to his mom, it was certainly worth a try!

SPEAKER: What I want you to know and what I want you to learn from that experience is that in this body, that will not happen to you. The human that is caring for you now will never do that.

MAXIMUS: Yes, I understand that.

SPEAKER: And she will protect you from whatever that was.

MAXIMUS: Yes, I understand. There were other lives [in which] it hadn't happened, but those three—that's why this is happening.

SPEAKER: That makes a lot of sense, though. Thank you for looking into that. It makes sense why you're afraid now.

MAXIMUS: Yes. When I hear the sound, it's like I said, *a switch.*

SPEAKER: Sure. Of course it is. What I'd like for you to try to do now— energetically—for me please, is, I want you to allow that to move out of your body and to be released from your energetic field. That phenomenon, that remembrance, any residual energy from those three incidents, I want you to allow that to flow out of your body now. Allow it to flow down into Mother Earth, and Mother Earth will transform that. Allow that energy to flow out of your body. Any remembrance of that will not disturb you, in any way, any longer. That energy was from a prior life and does not need to affect your current physical life. And I want your Higher Self to tell me when that is complete, please.

As I said those words, slowly and methodically, Maximus's body (through Will) began to relax, as he worked to release the traumatic energy from his field. This process took several minutes; eventually, I continued with words of encouragement...

SPEAKER: You're doing a beautiful job!

MAXIMUS: I feel it's moved on.

SPEAKER: Beautiful! Maximus, you did such a great job! Thank you so much. I believe now that you're going to be able to move forward without that trauma attached any longer. How do you feel about that?

MAXIMUS: I feel okay. I feel hopeful!

SPEAKER: Hopeful is good!

MAXIMUS: There's a part of me, still, that I'm nervous if I hear another sound, but I guess I'll just have to see.

SPEAKER: I want you to hold that intent.

MAXIMUS: I feel okay, I do. And I felt something move through.

SPEAKER: Good! I want you to know that your mom will make every effort to prevent any noises anyway, because it can be disturbing regardless, and your mom is there to protect you and keep you from any harm, all right?

MAXIMUS: Yes.

SPEAKER: Good! Now that we look back, do you think all of that trauma was causing some of the anxiety day to day? Perhaps each day you were nervous that something like that could happen?

MAXIMUS: Yes, I think that would make sense.

SPEAKER: So maybe your daily anxiety will reduce, as well.

MAXIMUS: It very well might. I actually do feel a bit more relaxed now.

SPEAKER: I'm very excited for you now moving forward. Do you think that was causing some of your barking, when you would bark in the house? Were you barking because you were anxious? What were you barking about?

MAXIMUS: That's an interesting question, because some of it I'm sure was. I hear noises, and I want to alert somebody that there's something around. But other times, I bark because I want the attention. I want somebody to be around. I want to be with someone. I want to be with my mom.

SPEAKER: I see, and what was your assignment with your mom, Maximus? Tell me about that.

MAXIMUS: Interesting...to be her protector. To watch over her. That's interesting! That's what I was [in those lives], too. I was the humans' protector there, too. It's just to alert and allow, just to be around her and step alongside her when she's out doing things, and letting other animals know not to get too close, and to watch over the house when she's not there.

SPEAKER: Beautiful, thank you! Is there anything else your mom needs to know before we close?

MAXIMUS: No. This has been wonderful! I had no idea. I'm seeing things like I'd be dreaming, but yet I'm able to tell you and tell my mom things. I'm really going to try to make sure this doesn't happen anymore. I do feel a bit more relaxed and a bit more calm inside. I do thank you, Mom, for allowing me to do this. I know we're going to understand each other much more than we ever have. I do love you, and I thank you! I just want to be by you.

PART III

HONEYBEES

We're here for you

T he honeybees were the first animal collective Will and I connected with. As I mentioned in the Introduction, I had wanted to chat with them about their honey. The bees were lovely creatures to speak with; their energy was calm and soothing, their words unassuming. In fact, their demeanor was in stark contrast to the wasps, the collective we channeled immediately afterwards. This is not to imply that the wasps were unkind; rather, they were much more matter-of-fact. That being said, the bees themselves were (apparently) not terribly enamored with the wasps, as detailed in the foreword.

The conversation with the bees and wasps reinforced how vital the relationship is between humans and animals. Rather than taking them for granted, as we all do from time to time, humanity must reevaluate—and take seriously—the many ways in which animals support human life; this is particularly true with regard to the insect population. If for no other reason than our own livelihood, it is imperative that we find better ways to support the animals with whom we share this planet—their habitats and their way of life.

According to researchers, the insect population as a whole has been declining by 2.5 percent each year. Honeybees, which pollinate fifteen billion dollars' worth of crops every year in the Unites States alone, have also been decreasing in number—a staggering forty percent of their colonies were lost during a single winter, between 2018 and 2019. Some scientists believe that the insect die-offs are an indication that Earth is entering its sixth mass extinction.

Regardless of how you feel about them, insects—particularly honeybees—are necessary for human life. Without them, we will perish. But even more than that, all animals embody a wisdom that comes directly from Source. They are here to teach us, to show us better ways to live. It would behoove mankind to pay attention.

HONEYBEE COLLECTIVE: We are present with you.

SPEAKER: Thank you. I just heard a humming, was that you all?

HONEYBEE COLLECTIVE: Yes

SPEAKER: That was amazing, wow! Thank you. You seem pleased to be here.

HONEYBEE COLLECTIVE: It's interesting to be here and connected to this individual as we are.

SPEAKER: It is interesting, and it's very much appreciated, so that we might get a message out to humanity about the bee collective. First off, is there anything you'd like for humans to know about bees?

HONEYBEE COLLECTIVE: Don't be fearful of us. Don't have any worry about us. Don't be scared. We will not harm you. We mean very well. We will protect our hive, we will protect those things that are valuable to us, but we'll never harm just to harm. We're here to provide you with the abundant riches that we have, albeit small at times. You have to understand that the wonderful thing that we can provide to you, our honey, our source of energy...think of it as, a bit of the sun and all of the glorious flowers of your planet all brought together in one little drop. It holds so much! It holds an understanding; it holds a healing; it holds energy, all within that little drop. So I hope you understand that it may be delicate, it may be something that is out of reach at times, but we'll always provide it for you.

SPEAKER: We are very appreciative of that delicacy that you provide. Do you understand—do the bees understand how critical they are to the lives of human beings?

HONEYBEE COLLECTIVE: Yes. It's not just the humans that it's critical to. We provide so much more, on so many other levels...for the flowers, for all the other animals, for the planet. There's so much more that takes place than you could understand. Each of our hives that we have, whether they're taken care of by the humans or we have our hives in the trees or anywhere else, it's a glorious center of energy! It's like a crystal ball full of energy, all wrapped up, all in one. The healing that it has, the vibration that it puts off transforms everything around it. I understand how critical we are, but we don't think of it that way. We have a job. We have a mission. That's what we are concerned with, fulfilling our mission, fulfilling our job, to provide that to you.

SPEAKER: Thank you, that was beautiful! So speaking of the honey you provide, I know there are some humans who don't eat animal products and feel it is unfair to take the honey from you. How do you feel about that? Can you help us to understand?

HONEYBEE COLLECTIVE: That may be difficult to explain. We understand our mission, we understand what we are to provide, and that's what we provide. Whether or not someone decides that it is their choice to either take it or not, that is theirs—it's not our decision. That is theirs. We cannot change that decision point, but we will always be there to provide it. For one, if they don't take it, then someone else will and [will] be utilizing it. For us, it doesn't make a difference. We're ok with that.

SPEAKER: Thank you for that. So if we do take the honey and use it, we're not depriving you in any way or harming you in any way?

HONEYBEE COLLECTIVE: No, there's plenty, plenty for us to have. We use it as much as we can. But that's why we make so much. We understand how much we have to make. We make just enough to provide for ourselves, and then the rest [is] for humans and other animals.

SPEAKER: Thank you for that! That's good to know. You know, humans are quite amazed at your aerodynamics. Your body is quite large, comparatively speaking, relative to your wings. I think humans are pretty confounded and fascinated that you can get off the ground and fly so easily. Do you have anything you want to say about that?

HONEYBEE COLLECTIVE: Hmm. We've never given it thought. That's quite difficult to comprehend. I think if we were to think about this difference, maybe we wouldn't fly. But all we know is, given enough space, we can fly wherever we wish. We don't think about how we're built. We just think about where we need to be and how to get back.

SPEAKER: Wow! That's an amazingly profound statement you just made, that if you thought about it, you might never fly. That is so important for humans to understand—that when we think too much, it prohibits us from acting. Wow!

HONEYBEE COLLECTIVE: Yes, I think that's very true. If we were to sit in our hive and think about things, about whether we could fly or not, I would imagine many of us wouldn't fly, because we'd be worried that we'd fall out of the sky.

SPEAKER: Wow! That sounds so simple but it's so amazing! Thank you for bringing that to our attention. That is unbelievable, thank you. So, bees have really mastered being able to work together as a collective, and humans could really learn from that. Do you have any advice for us about that?

HONEYBEE COLLECTIVE: There is no difference amongst each one of us—we're all the same. But we all have our unique mission; we all have our unique job. We all do the same thing, but yet, each thing is just a bit different. We don't look at each other as being different. We all look at each other as what we have to do. And if one isn't doing what they're supposed to do, we have our way of being able to get them to... um....maybe do something different, but we don't look at them any differently.

It's just that, when we are transformed into our "bee" Self, we know what we have to do at that point—whether that's tend to the hive, and that's all we do, or whether [it's that] we fly out and bring back pollen, take care of the queen, or even just to sit and cool the hive. We all have our mission. But yet, we don't look upon each other as an individual. We don't look upon each other as doing an "individual" thing. We're part of a...you said it...collective. We do things together. We don't think about what we look like.

SPEAKER: And so none of the jobs are considered preferable to any other, correct?

HONEYBEE COLLECTIVE: No, they're all equally as powerful, yes.

SPEAKER: And do those jobs change over the lifespan of the bee or do you come in doing one role for your entire life?

HONEYBEE COLLECTIVE: You may have a specific role, but if there's a need to be filled, you know how to do that, as well. You will fill in if you need to. Sometimes it happens, but for the most part, you fulfill your role for the length that you're here.

SPEAKER: Do different types of bees gravitate towards different types of flowers or do you just go towards whatever is in your environment?

HONEYBEE COLLECTIVE: Whatever's around our area. We have a big area that we have to cover, and as long as there are flowers there, that's what pollen [we will bring] back.

SPEAKER: Pretty amazing! Do the ones that fly out consider their job to be more dangerous than the ones that stay close to the hive?

HONEYBEE COLLECTIVE: I don't believe any of us think of anything as being dangerous. No, it's not a thought that we have. We just know what our mission is. Our mission is to do this, whether that's to fly miles to get what we need or stay close. Staying close can be just as dangerous. There are plenty of things that are close that could do harm to us, just as [much as] going out and collecting pollen. So we don't give it much thought. It's just the same as we don't give it thought of whether we can fly or not. There's no need to think about what's dangerous. It's just, *"What's our mission?"* and *"How do we accomplish it?"*

SPEAKER: Another valuable piece of wisdom for humans. Thank you, it has been very enlightening to speak with you! Is there anything else you'd like to communicate to humanity before you go?

HONEYBEE COLLECTIVE: Just to be peaceful with us. Just to be with the understanding that we will not provide you harm. We're only there to provide you good and comfort. If you're patient enough, if you're relaxed enough, and you are around us, we may even land on you. We're always just wanting to connect. We're here for *you*, just as much as you are here for us.

19

WASPS

Each insect that is here has its own mission, has its own purpose

The bees and wasps were the first two animal collectives we spoke with on our new journey. The wasps were the first to make me cry. I think it was because I knew that *they knew* that I have never hesitated to kill them when I've seen them around, particularly since we have so many of them that set up their homes around our house and pool. Their stings hurt! And they multiply so darn fast! But in that moment, the wasps KNEW me. I couldn't hide; I couldn't pretend. I guess this is how judgement day will feel—even if we feel justified in our actions (killing wasps), we will have to reconcile with those actions. After that conversation, I knew things would never, could never be the same.

Imagine that you are a grade school bully. One day, you decide to invite that scrawny kid, your victim, to the picnic table at recess for a conversation about life. Surprisingly, he agrees. The conversation is great! From a completely neutral standpoint, the little kid explains to you the nature of the universe. You appreciate him being so open, so vulnerable. Although everything he says rings true, you know that tomorrow, when you both arrive back at school, you will bully him again. Or, will you?

Once I started connecting with these animals—all animals—in this way, things changed. Although there have been occasions, since my wasp conversation, when I have had to kill a small nest or an individual wasp, it has no longer been without contemplation and consideration. I took their words to heart. I now understand life from the wasp's perspective. I respect them, even if I can't always live with them.

WASP COLLECTIVE: We are here.

SPEAKER: Thank you for your presence with us. What is your role or mission on Earth?

WASP COLLECTIVE: The primary role or mission that you are asking, is one to watch out for and build our small community, small collective of other wasps. It is to build a colony, to establish our presence, and raise our young, and enjoy the things of *this* planet. To be present here, yes.

SPEAKER: Other than that experience, living in community, is there a mission of service to planet Earth or humanity or other animals?

WASP COLLECTIVE: All insects and all animals, as well as you humans, have that mission for the planet or Mother Earth. Yes, we too, provide back to Mother Earth, in very small ways. We are not like some other insects that build large colonies or large hives, but we do help pollinate; not as much as some of the bees do. Again, we too, collect nectar, pollen, but in very small ways, just enough to take care of *our* young. But in doing so, it's helping with the plants that we pollinate. So that, in itself, is taking care of Mother Nature.

SPEAKER: Wasps tend to have a bad reputation with humans due to your seemingly aggressive nature. Can you speak to that?

WASP COLLECTIVE: Yes, we're very defensive of our small colonies, our hives. And yes, we have been aggressive towards the humans or other animals if they disrupt our hive. It's merely just a defensive thing. We will, yes, as you call it, attack if we need to. But really, what you must understand is we only attack when we know that we're going to be harmed in some way. We also sense the vibrations coming off of other beings, other animals, other things...more so than many other insects. And when we sense that fear—[when the human is] afraid—generally, when that happens, it means they're going to do something to us. That's when we will make sure that they do not.

SPEAKER: Thank you for that explanation. But one time, I was stung on the pinky finger while floating and meditating in my pool. I was definitely not sending off a fearful vibe or disturbing a hive.

WASP COLLECTIVE: One must understand this, that when we come in contact or we happen to find ourselves in the presence of humans, we have been so conditioned, for the most part, that humans will try to destroy our way of life. So when we sense that we are around a human or we are near a human, we will be in a defensive posture. And it may have been that, yes, you may have been in a very relaxed state, but when this particular wasp may have landed on you, it knew that it was a human, and its reaction is to defend itself. It may have been by mistake, knowing that you may have been in a meditative state, but this wasp, all he knew, or she knew, was that it must defend—it's a human.

SPEAKER: Thank you for explaining your perspective. Can you speak to murder hornets? Hornets fall under the wasp category.

WASP COLLECTIVE: Yes, most humans do put the hornets under the same category as wasps. They are extremely different. They are even more aggressive than wasps. They're very territorial and very defensive of their surroundings. *We* tend not to even mess with hornets, as they are very, very aggressive! This *murder hornet* that you speak of, I am not familiar with. It is not something that I understand. There are many species of hornets that, yes, they are very, very aggressive and will attack anything in their area to clear it out so that they can "take hold" of that area. So it may be very similar to what you are experiencing.

SPEAKER: Very interesting! How can humans better coexist with you?

WASP COLLECTIVE: I think this advice would be for any human-to-insect contact: to open yourself up and allow your vibration to speak to any insect, calmly and respectfully. To allow yourself the understanding that you can communicate with us, as well as with any other insect. And in doing so, we may relax just a bit. You have to understand that we are a bit conditioned to the understanding that many humans will try to destroy us, but through your persistence and your calm manner, you may be able to speak with us and allow us to know that you're not going to do harm.

SPEAKER: What if we have to destroy your home due to having pets, children, allergies, etc.?

WASP COLLECTIVE: One, it would be the easiest if you could allow us to be and have that understanding that would be built. But we understand that, yes, there are some humans that...they do more damage than good. So in that case, I ask that if you are going to remove one of our nests, that you do it quickly, before it is too big and we have too many losses. If it is too big, we ask that you wait, and then we will be gone. We allow ourselves a bit of time to understand that there is a new birth that takes place, but once they are all brought out, then they each seek their own place to have a hive. You can wait until it's cooler to remove that nest. There will still be some loss, but it won't be as great. I ask that you respect that.

SPEAKER: Thank you for that information. It is very helpful! Is there anything else you would like to share with humanity?

WASP COLLECTIVE: Just understand that each animal, each being, each insect that is here has its own mission, has its own purpose. None of them are here to inflict intentional harm, but because of circumstances, and how they are conditioned, they may do so, in defense of *their* home. But if you have a relationship with them, and you can speak to them, and you can do this calmly and respectfully, I believe that some of that would be taken care of and lessened. All I ask is that you just do that.

SPEAKER: Thank you very much for your presence today!

20

WHALES, DOLPHINS, AND MANATEES

Water is the medium by which all communication takes place

L iving on the South Carolina coast, Will and I enjoy taking our pontoon boat out on the various local waterways, where we almost always see dolphins—we've even had several encounters with manatees. I can honestly say, the sightings never get old! I'm confident that I'm not alone in my admiration of these beautiful beings. Very often, when a pod of dolphins is spotted, other boaters can't help but stop...all of us enthusiastically pointing and staring. Time seems to stand still when we are in their presence—we somehow forget all of our grievances and forge a bond with one another, united in our overwhelming love for these incredible animals. Although I don't have many opportunities to glimpse whales in their natural habitat, they too, have the power to inspire awe.

What is it about these sea creatures that mesmerizes us? That brings out the best in us? Do we envy their sense of freedom? Their innocence? Their intelligence? For eons, humans have enjoyed an inexplicable bond with whales and dolphins, in particular, and the collective speaks about that below. (Spoiler alert: It's all about the heart!) Ultimately, it all comes back to love. The kind of love that unites and connects us, causing us to transcend our faults, our frailties, our humanness. Love is the power we feel when we encounter the whales, dolphins, and manatees.

～

WHALE, DOLPHIN, MANATEE COLLECTIVE: We are present with you.

SPEAKER: Thank you very much for your presence. Is there something you'd like to share with humanity at this time?

WHALE, DOLPHIN, MANATEE COLLECTIVE: Know that you as humans are not too far removed in energy and thought from us. Though physically, yes, we are quite different, [our] energetic and thought process is quite similar, and to a certain extent, far superior. We have many different ways of communicating with you.

What you have to understand is, you have yet to fully open your understanding, your thoughts, your way of thinking about life, to fully comprehend what is possible with your existence. Though we may be perceived as slow and incapable, we are far more superior than you think. We have a far greater command of existence than you understand. So, do not take that lightly. Explore deeper within your understanding, your capability, your thought processes, to unlock what the potential is. There is so much more there, and you would be amazed what you can achieve!

SPEAKER: Thank you for that. I agree with you. Because of our energetic similarity, do you think that's why humans have such an affinity for you...particularly dolphins?

WHALE, DOLPHIN, MANATEE COLLECTIVE: It is the energetic exchange that takes place when you are near. When any human is in contact with any one of us, there is a greater cognitive connection. A telepathic pathway is opened, a direct connection from your heart to our heart, and that is why you feel drawn or akin to us. So whenever you can experience this, take the time to fully involve yourself. This will only help to grow your understanding of experience.

SPEAKER: Thank you. I personally do try to take advantage of every opportunity to tune in to the dolphins when we're out on the water. Whales not so much, because I'm not there where you exist. But I've tried to call on them mentally to come close to the boat so that I could communicate with and appreciate them. I haven't had much luck. Is that just because of the way that I'm communicating, or is it simply their free will?

WHALE, DOLPHIN, MANATEE COLLECTIVE: Though you are calling upon us, though you are sending that signal out, we are quite playful, and we like to play a bit of a game. Though you may not see us right close to where you want us to be, we are there. You have to understand, your thoughts travel quite far in the water. Your energy travels quite far in the water. So just because you don't see us, we may be right below where you're at. We like to play! We're very playful, especially when it comes to the humans. We like to play around them. We understand how excited the humans get, but sometimes, we want to stay just below the surface to keep the intrigue in play.

SPEAKER: Thank you for that! What is your role as a collective on the planet at this time?

WHALE, DOLPHIN, MANATEE COLLECTIVE: The role of the whales is one of master teacher. Master of all understandings of existence. You would say a master of the Universe. We are the ones that convey the understanding of all things to other sea life. We are the teachers for that existence. We are there to convey that energy throughout the planet. We are there when called upon to help heal certain areas.

The role of a dolphin is one to be playful, to understand play in life, to understand how important it is to play, to be expressive, to dance in the water, and to express that to all the other animals, to allow them to understand that it is okay to be yourself. No matter what you look like, no matter how you are placed here, find time to play. Forget about what you are and just play! Allow that energy to surround you, to make your existence better.

The role of the manatee is one of compassion and gratitude. We are there just to take our time and have gratitude for all of the things that are provided for us. We are filled with the gratitude that we have an existence here amongst the humans and [are] provided for in such a wonderful fashion. We also provide the compassion to those that are ailing, to those that are sick, to those that are energetically down. You can think of us as the nurse to tend to all the wounds, whether it is the planet, or the humans, or any other animal. We send that energy out. The healing energy that we provide travels throughout all of the planet.

SPEAKER: Thank you! That's beautiful, and we're so grateful to have you all! We understand that you all are very intelligent creatures. Do humans give you enough credit? It sounds like perhaps we don't.

WHALE, DOLPHIN, MANATEE COLLECTIVE: It is difficult for the humans to comprehend the extent of our knowing, our presence. So you are correct when you say that the humans do not give us enough credit. There are those that do, but for the most part, we are taken for granted that we exist only to exist; [that] we are just another animal upon this planet. But we've been here much longer than you have, and we will remain here much longer than you will. We have an understanding, a universal understanding of existence, and we understand what we are here for.

SPEAKER: Thank you for that. My understanding, I think, at least with dolphins, is that you all were seeded on Earth when it was created—purposefully—from another planet. Is that correct?

WHALE, DOLPHIN, MANATEE COLLECTIVE: There is a truth in this, yes. You have to understand that as a planet, [Earth] is quite young. The existence of its inhabitants is quite young compared to many others. And yes, at a particular point, not only our species but many others were brought to this planet. In a particular form, the human species, as well, was brought to this planet, to begin to populate this planet.

So yes, in a fashion, we were put here, seeded, as you speak of. But as time goes on, it is just merely an understanding. There are very few remnants left of that existence, very few pieces that have been carried on and on, in existence here on this planet.

What you must understand is those that have been placed here did not look like what you perceive them to be now. They had a much different appearance. This is, as you call it, the evolutionary change that takes place. As environmental aspects change, its inhabitants must keep up. So at the time at which those were placed here, your planet looked much different. Our existence looked much different. That is why we say that now there is only a small bit of remnant that remains of that existence.

SPEAKER: That makes sense, thank you. In terms of the manatee, humanity can learn gratitude and compassion, and from the dolphin, we can learn playfulness and the ability to be ourselves. What should humanity learn from the whales? What are the whales to teach us?

WHALE, DOLPHIN, MANATEE COLLECTIVE: Your existence is merely temporary here, but your understanding, your thought, remains. Though you are in a temporary existence along with many others here, your thoughts and your understandings and your teachings will remain from existence to existence. So what takes place in this life is not only a representation of what *has* taken place, but it will be a representation of what *will* take place.

That is not to say to change things but to have an understanding of what takes place. It is for you to *choose* what you wish to do, but understanding the universal knowing that it is all carried on from point to point, just in a different existence, would help your human species to know what has taken place, to help what will take place.

SPEAKER: Thank you. I don't think we have an accurate representation or understanding of what has taken place. I don't think we've found that truth yet.

WHALE, DOLPHIN, MANATEE COLLECTIVE: The truth lies within each of you. It is how far back you wish to explore. There are many, and this is for all—animals, insects, humans—all inhabitants. There is a portion which you do not remember, but you have [the] full existence in you. You understand all that has taken place before your time here, but there is a portion that is yet to be opened. That book is not to be opened. Many try to explore these existences, and it is possible, but it is only a select few individuals that hold the key to the full understanding of their existence. But to have a glimpse into the past to change the mindset of the present, to change a life in the future, that is all that is asked.

SPEAKER: That makes sense. Thank you. So it is very important for each of us to go within and to explore all of that?

WHALE, DOLPHIN, MANATEE COLLECTIVE: This is correct.

SPEAKER: Beautiful. Is there anything else that you would like to convey to humanity?

WHALE, DOLPHIN, MANATEE COLLECTIVE: You inhabit only one small portion of this planet. There is much more to explore. Being in the presence of any water will help you explore this. Water is the medium by which all communication takes place. The vibration sent out through a body of water travels all around the planet, and it remains there. So, all that has been taught over the period of existence on this planet still remains in that water. But you have to be willing to open yourself up to [that] understanding and be willing to accept what comes in and have that as a knowing for your future.

SPEAKER: Wow, thank you! I should've known to ask about the water and its importance, so I appreciate you adding that. Anything else?

WHALE, DOLPHIN, MANATEE COLLECTIVE: Nothing at this time.

SPEAKER: Thank you so very much for coming in to speak with us today.

WHALE, DOLPHIN, MANATEE COLLECTIVE: Thank you.

21

SPIDERS

Sit still and wait

I ncluding spiders in this book was a no-brainer for a couple of reasons. First and foremost, millions (billions?) of people find spiders terrifying! They are probably among the most loathed creatures on the planet. There are memes galore on Facebook—you know the ones—people who would rather burn down their home than deal with a spider. Spider webs adorn haunted houses, while women who murder their spouses are referred to as a "black widow." Movies like *Arachnophobia* (1990), *Tarantula* (1955), and *Kingdom of the Spiders* (1977)—and countless others—have served to exacerbate our collective fear.

Personally, I find spiders intriguing. Daddy long-legs, banana spiders, jumping spiders...they come in such an amazing assortment of colors, shapes, and sizes! When we lived in south Texas, we adopted two pet tarantulas, which were native to that area. After dark, it was quite common to spot them scurrying across the road. In spite of their reputation, spiders are actually quite magical. The spider, with her two-lobed body and eight legs, represents infinite possibilities, limitlessness.

The spider's web has been used for eons as a metaphor for many significant concepts—in philosophy, education, religion...you name it. It's even been speculated that the spider weaved the first primordial alphabet within her web, helping humanity move from petroglyphs to letters.[1] Naturally, I was curious to speak with the spiders themselves, to understand their perspective—not only about how we perceive them but what we can learn from them.

～

SPIDER COLLECTIVE: We are present.

SPEAKER: Thank you so much for your presence today. I find spiders to be fascinating! There are so many varieties, and you're all very unique, but unfortunately many humans are quite fearful of you. What would you like to say to us?

SPIDER COLLECTIVE: Just as fearful as you are of us, we are of you. We're quite small, and we understand that. We understand that we have a purpose. We have things that we have to do, just like you have things to do, as well. We try not to disturb your world, as best as we can, but we understand that there are some that do not like our presence, and they're unaware of the benefits of what we can do. Yes, they do remove us, and we understand that. It's just part of the experience.

With many of the insects, we understand that our life is quite short. It could be a day. It could be a month. It could be a couple of months. In that time, we have to do everything we can. Think of it as if you knew your life was only three months long, how much you would want to do in those three months. We have to do a lot in that short amount of time, and we understand that if it's our time to move on, whether it's by the human, or by an animal, or by some other means, we understand that. And we're okay with that.

SPEAKER: Beautiful! Thank you for that opening message. You mentioned that we don't often *"understand your benefit."* Can you explain your benefit to humanity?

SPIDER COLLECTIVE: Most importantly, we do keep some of the bugs away from where you are. So if you see our webs near your house, it's because we're trying to keep some of the bugs away from you, some of the different bugs. We can't keep them all away, but we try our best to do that. But the other thing is our web. The humans like to enjoy our webs and all the different shapes and different sizes. It allows them to look at it and realize how masterful we are, and how intricate it is, and so delicate. They look upon it as maybe a symbol for their life—how delicate it is and how connected it is.

SPEAKER: I agree with you. It is very intricate and beautiful! Often, we like to stop and show our appreciation for that, yes. We also use your web as a metaphor for many of our concepts—spiritual concepts, human concepts. Can you speak to that for us?

SPIDER COLLECTIVE: You would think that when we build our webs, it's just from memory, and it's what we do...it's something that we remember to do, and it's just built that way. But [that's] not quite the right way to think about it. Each place we do a web, we're actually building it to connect with the energy that's there. As we build a web, if it's in one location, it might look a certain way, and if we move it to another location, it may be slightly different. That's because we're sensing the energy and the vibration that's in that area. We're building it to not only catch the insects but [to] help catch the vibration and the frequency that's there, the energy that's there. It's helping us. As the energy gets caught in the web, it changes a bit, and then it moves on. So we're helping move the energy around just a little bit differently.

SPEAKER: Wow, that's fascinating! I had no idea. Then, what could humans gain from tuning in to that energy of the web as we pass by?

SPIDER COLLECTIVE: Just take a moment and step in front of the web and just look at it, and understand that it's not a "thing," but it actually is something that *does* something. Tune in to that. Many people do sense the energy there with the webs, but understand that it's kind of like —I don't know how to explain it, but as it moves through the web, it comes out the other side just a bit different. Just take [a] moment and sense that.

SPEAKER: Wow! Thank you for that. One of the other metaphors of the web is the interconnectedness of everything and that because they're so sensitive, if something tweaks one side of the web, it is felt all the way on the other side because of the interconnectedness. Would you like to speak to that?

SPIDER COLLECTIVE: Yes. It's interesting because that's how we know we've captured something. We know exactly what string or what intersection it is, and we know immediately where to go. It's interesting that the humans can't sense that with themselves. They're connected, too, in a way like that.

With all energy, it's all connected together. Whether you're a human, or an insect, or an animal, all the energy is connected together. It's difficult to understand that a human cannot sense that change in the energy or change in where it's being affected in one area. It's very common for us, even if there are multiple webs that are all connected together on the same plant or same location but from different spiders; we sense even when there's an insect in someone else's web. We sense that across all of the webs. But we understand that that isn't our web.

I think if you could understand and fully get into the energy stream of your existence, you would be able to sense all the different vibrations all around you and how they're affecting you and other people, and when another person is affected by something, how you would be affected by it and so on.

SPEAKER: You're right. That would be very helpful if we all tuned in that way. Before we close, is there a lesson that spiders are here to teach humanity?

SPIDER COLLECTIVE: Just be more sensitive. Even though we have this beautiful web that we use to sustain our life and connect things together, it's just being sensitive to what's around you, the vibrations that are around you. Every little thing causes a vibration, a change in the vibration, and you have to be sensitive to it to understand it. You have to be in tune with each of the vibrations, and you have to sit still, waiting until that vibration changes. Then you'll understand more about it. But if you're moving around and you're constantly doing repairs to your web and moving around and changing things, you won't have time to feel the vibration and the changes in things. You have to sit still and wait.

SPEAKER: Ah, yes. Wise words. Thank you so very much for coming in today.

22

SNAKES

Have patience to know which opportunity is the right one

Like spiders, the snake is another animal that strikes fear in the hearts of many. It doesn't help that snakes have been used throughout history as a universal symbol representing death, destruction, and evil. As with many of our belief systems, these negative stereotypes are often passed along through our family and friends or perpetuated by the media.

In the metaphysical world, snakes are actually powerful, positive symbols of rebirth, transformation, immortality, and healing. Whether we "like" them or not, *all* animals are valuable, *all* animals have purpose, and *all* animals are connected to us through the web of life. To me, it was important that this book give voice to some of those "undesirables," the animals that are traditionally despised or disregarded, so that we may grow to appreciate what they are here to teach us.

SNAKE COLLECTIVE: We are present with you.

SPEAKER: Thank you for being present. Do you have a message for humanity that you'd like to share first? Is there something we need to know?

SNAKE COLLECTIVE: Do not be afraid of us. Do not be afraid of any of us. We understand there are many of us that do cause harm, but do not be afraid of us. You have to understand what we bring to you. You have to understand what energy we bring to you. There is much protection for the land that we live upon that we bring to you. We surround and inhabit your land in order to protect it from those animals that wish to come in and partake of food that you are growing, those animals that wish to cause harm to your buildings and do damage to things that you wish they weren't doing. We are your guardians of your property, but we also bring in the energy of growth and change, rebirth to all things that we come in contact with. So do not be afraid of us. Do not be afraid of any of us. We are here for you.

SPEAKER: Thank you so much. I understand that. I know that many humans are very afraid of snakes, partly because you can actually kill a human and partly due to unfortunate propaganda throughout time.

SNAKE COLLECTIVE: If you speak to us, and if you understand that we're there, we will honor that. If you happen to cross paths with us, do not be alarmed. Just breathe in our energy, thank us for being there, and allow us to go about our way as you are to go about yours. We will not cross you anymore.

SPEAKER: So we can speak to you?

SNAKE COLLECTIVE: You can speak to all animals, whether you see them or not. This is what is possible for all animals. They understand. As you speak the words you speak, they hear, they sense, they feel. So as you speak to them, even though they are not there with you, they understand.

SPEAKER: Beautiful! Thank you. Tell me about the incarnation process from your experience, when you come into a body.

SNAKE COLLECTIVE: Before coming into any body, it is as if all of us, all energy, all animals, are all together in one place. We understand what we have been and are looking forward to what we will be. And when it is time, we are then provided the understanding of what we will be. If it is a snake, then we become a snake. If it is a bird, we become a bird. If it is something else, we become that.

There are different points along the way that some of the animal energy is then assigned to humans [as a pet, for example]. But all in all, it is all part of a placement process. It is all part of one whole Source of energy and bits and pieces that are broken off and put into a specific animal. We understand that animal's role at that point. We understand, once we are placed into that animal, our role. We also understand that our existence may be quite quick, but that is why we understand the animal energy. We understand that we have to take part in each different type of animal energy. It is all a better part of an understanding of all animal existence. It is part of the understanding of, as you call it, the circle of life.

SPEAKER: Thank you; that makes sense. When you say *"understand your role,"* each animal has a specific role, and you spoke of yours earlier. Is that correct?

SNAKE COLLECTIVE: This is correct.

SPEAKER: Beautiful, thank you. In closing, what can humans learn from the snake collective?

SNAKE COLLECTIVE: Patience. Snakes are quite patient. We understand what it is to hunt, but we are not as successful as you may think, so we wait and we wait until the right opportunity. So we are patient for our meals, and when we take our meal, we are very, very thankful, as that meal will sustain us for quite some time. Do not overlook any opportunity, but have the patience to know which one is the right opportunity.

SPEAKER: Very profound! Thank you for those wise words. Is there anything else we need to know or you need to share with us, please?

SNAKE COLLECTIVE: Do not be afraid. We will do you no harm as long as you understand our placement. We understand yours. Communicate with us, and we will understand.

SPEAKER: Beautiful! Thank you so very much for coming in today.

RATS

Give thanks

This conversation came about when a client, Betty, contacted us with an urgent concern. The building in which she worked had become overrun with rats. Rat bait was being set out by the building owners, but Betty's empathic nature compelled her to find a solution that didn't involve killing the rats. She had already trapped a good number of them and released them into the woods, but they were reproducing way too fast. Catch and release wasn't a sustainable solution.

Betty had heard about our pet channelings and contacted us about scheduling a session for her own pets. As we emailed back and forth, she shared her rat dilemma with us and wondered if we could somehow help. We decided that, at the end of her pet session, we would call upon the rats to see what they had to say. We knew it wouldn't be as easy as asking them to leave and then watching them pack their bags. After all, the animal kingdom doesn't operate on the whim of the human—every animal species has its purpose and mission. The fact that they disturb or inconvenience us isn't their primary concern (although it's not their goal, either...it is often simply a byproduct of their coexistence with us). That being said, all animals understand the need to coexist—in harmony if possible—so, we wanted to hear their perspective.

RAT COLLECTIVE: We are present.

SPEAKER: Welcome! Thank you for your presence. Do you have an opening statement?

RAT COLLECTIVE: Most of the humans understand us for a reason other than pleasant. We are looked upon as being less than, inadequate, diseased. But what must be understood...we have an equal place in all things, just as all animals do. We mean no harm by, as you say, destroying, or infesting, or causing damage. But there is a greater purpose in this. For what you have in this place is suitable for our home—we must make a home for ourselves just as you must make a home for yourselves. There is no difference between the human taking a tree or any other natural product and making their home. We don't have the ability to build a home such as yours, so we find suitable items, and it just happens to be that where *we* are and *you* are, provide that for us. We understand that it is damaging to what you have. But that is the risk we are willing to take to provide a home for our family. There are different things you can do, but we will always find a way to build our home.

SPEAKER: Thank you for sharing your perspective. We wanted to speak to you because you are currently inhabiting Betty's building, and your presence there is causing difficulty. The building owners are trying to kill you, because you could damage the building. Betty would like to come up with a different solution, if possible. She tried to relocate many of you. What would you like to say about all of that?

RAT COLLECTIVE: We understand that you (Betty) are concerned about our lives and our existence, where others are not so concerned. They will do anything to eliminate us from the area. What you must understand is, *that* is our understanding of life. That is why we have extremely large families, because we know that part of our life could come to an end very quickly. But there are always others that have moved beyond our home to start a home of their own. So the cycle is very quick. We understand this, and we accept this. So there is nothing to be overly concerned about. There are plenty of us to inhabit wherever we wish. There are ways to stop the reproduction rate, but this would cause harm to many of us. What you have to understand is, we understand that. That is our choice for this existence. We know that this is a possibility for our existence, and we have to take that into account when we establish a new home.

What we would ask is for [you] to sit in our area, sit with us, and quietly express [your] concerns, and we will do our best to come to a compromise. But what we would also say is, there are certain actions you will have to take as well. You may have to move certain things away from us. You may have to remove those items that we wish to build our homes with. That is not to say that we will not remain there. We'll remain there, but we'll find another source that is suitable for us to build our homes. There is a way to coexist, but we have to have [an] equal understanding of what it [means] *to* coexist.

SPEAKER: Do you understand that poison bait traps have been set out?

RAT COLLECTIVE: We sense them, and we express that to many others, but there are those that have to understand that differently. That is their choice, their plan. Their life is what they have chosen, and if it's to end that way, that's the way they have selected.

We ask that you come to us and we will listen. We may not be present in front of you, but we will hear you. We will hear your words, and we will do our best to compromise. And I ask that, as you speak your words to us, you begin to listen to what we have to say to you. It is easy to hear these words, now, in front of you, but when you are in quiet with us, I ask that you listen to what we are saying. This is how we can, then, coexist together.

As I am speaking to you, *all* of the rats, *all* of the mice understand the words that are spoken. They also understand the words that are being received. They understand their place just as you understand *your* place. As [with] any animal, there is a coexistence that can take place, but a willingness to speak to one another must be there first. That is the lesson to understand.

SPEAKER: Thank you for that. What can you tell us about the differences between rats and mice?

RAT COLLECTIVE: It is just the location in which we inhabit. Mice are more...out in the woods and around other animals. Rats, we like to be around the humans. There is comfort in that. There are many more things that we can explore, eat, and enjoy. The mice are more free to roam and forage out in the wilderness and around other animals. They have a different type of life than we do.

SPEAKER: I find your use of the word *comfort*, in being around humans, interesting, given that most humans aren't very fond of rats.

RAT COLLECTIVE: This is correct, because they have been *taught* that we are not suitable. They are *taught* that we will provide them some sort of disease, some sort of discomfort. When in reality, yes, we may have different things with us, but in reality, we enjoy being around the humans. We enjoy their way of life, their food, their homes, and yes, unfortunately, you would perceive it as we are doing damage. But we enjoy their homes.

SPEAKER: Thank you for that explanation. What can humans learn from the rats and mice?

RAT COLLECTIVE: Just as I've expressed, there is no difference between how you build your home and how we build ours. We utilize the things that are abundant in our area. But what *we* do is we give thanks for those things to be in our area. Though it might be damaging to *your* items, we're thankful that they're present to give us our comfort, our home, our place of existence. I think the humans could do the same when they build their homes and they take the trees or the other items that it takes to build their home—to give thanks. Yes, many, I don't believe, do this. Everything is provided for a reason. Whether that's your food or your home. It's all provided for a reason. And you shall give thanks for that.

SPEAKER: Understood! Thank you so much for your presence with us today.

24

FIREFLIES

Enjoy each moment as it happens

Before connecting with the fireflies (aka lightning bugs), I had already spoken to a number of animal collectives and was just about ready to start compiling this book. But I wanted to chat with the entire animal kingdom, as a whole, to see if they had a general message to share with humanity, one that I could include in this project. (As a matter of fact, they did, and you can read their profound message in the afterword.)

During that conversation, I asked if there were any other animal collectives that really wanted to speak, any that I hadn't included yet. After all, with over 8.7 million animal species on the planet, it was quite a challenge to decide which animals to include! The animal kingdom instructed me to use my intuition...to connect with them and listen for guidance. I was told that my energy would draw in those that wished to participate.

That very evening, just after sundown, Will and I strolled down our driveway towards the road, enjoying the warm summer weather. All of a sudden, I saw a tiny flash of light out of the corner of my eye. I thought it was a firefly, but as I scanned the neighborhood, I couldn't detect any more twinkles. Not long before that "sighting," I had lamented the fact that the lightning bugs of my youth seemed to have disappeared. I rarely saw them in the yard anymore, most definitely not in the numbers I experienced as a child, when their light shows were a nightly spectacle.

It occurred to me that, perhaps, they simply wanted to get my attention. Maybe they were asking for a voice, because they had wisdom to share. I decided to trust my instinct and connect with them. Not surprisingly, their words were powerful! In fact, their message seemed to speak to me directly, reminding me that, if my first inclination was to doubt that I even saw a lightning bug that night, don't—just trust. Trust my intuition; trust that they were communicating with me.

FIREFLY COLLECTIVE: We are present.

SPEAKER: Thank you so much for your presence. I thought I saw a lightning bug the other evening. They're getting scarce lately. I got the sense that perhaps you wanted to speak. Is there something you'd like to share with us?

FIREFLY COLLECTIVE: Thank you for witnessing us. It is not that we are, as you say, becoming scarce. It's just that we're moving on to different locations, [so] that we can have a much better home. There is much that is changing all throughout that does not sustain us well, so we must find another location. There are those that still remain behind. They are there, trying to rejuvenate that area. But it is not necessary to worry too much, for we understand our time here is limited, and it is a short amount of time that we are here, so we must do what we can in that short amount of time.

When you see us, thank us, for the light that we give you is the light that you seek. You are seeking. You are wanting to understand. That little dot of light that we provide gives you hope, gives you a chance to look a little bit further. You may think that you're seeing something that isn't, but you are. Keep that as your perspective. When you think you see something, you actually are. Keep your eyes open and more will appear.

SPEAKER: Wow, what a very profound message! Thank you. I needed to hear that. When you say that you are relocating, do you mean to different geographic areas on the planet?

FIREFLY COLLECTIVE: Yes, different locations upon your planet— more sustainable for our existence.

SPEAKER: Thank you for that. I had read, though, that our scientists said that when lightning bugs' habitats are destroyed, they just disappear. They don't relocate like other animals. What do you have to say about that?

FIREFLY COLLECTIVE: It's difficult to explain that. When an area that we inhabit changes dramatically, the trees and the grass are no longer, there is nothing there to sustain us. Being that we have such a short span of time that we are present here in our physical existence, we do what we can.

If the geographic area is destroyed or changed in a way that doesn't sustain us, then we do not emerge the next year. Our young do not emerge. They understand this. For we as adults have a short span, and then we transition. We leave behind our young, our eggs, to then hatch. But if they know that there isn't a sustainable environment, they will not emerge. They will not hatch. They will not grow. And that, they understand. As they come into that egg, that larvae, they understand this. So they never emerge into that firefly.

SPEAKER: That makes sense. But as adults, if you sense that, you can relocate as adults? Is that what you're saying?

FIREFLY COLLECTIVE: Yes. If there's enough time to sustain our existence here. If we do emerge, and we are in our adult form and things begin to change, yes, we will begin to shift into another area so that we can then mate and then lay our young in preparation for the next year.

SPEAKER: Thank you for that explanation. That's helpful. You all are certainly fascinating! One of the most unique animals on planet Earth and very enjoyable to discover. I noticed that in certain geographic areas of our planet, you all synchronize your light flashes, which is quite amazing to behold. Why do you do this, or what does it mean?

FIREFLY COLLECTIVE: From our physical presence, it is our way of signaling to a mate. That is our way of being able to draw our mate in to us. And for your observance, it is quite unique. But there is another perspective to that. You must understand that from an energetic stand-point, it doesn't matter whether it is us or another insect or another animal; we all have an energetic purpose, an energetic connection.

When we are able to all, as you say, synchronize, you would believe it to be that we are all communicating together in order for us to emit our light together at the same time. In some aspect that is true. But what we are understanding it as, as we all gather, and we are all together in that location, we are all sensing the vibrational expression of that land, and we are then in communication with it. It is then we are expressing its vibration through us, through the light that we emit. If it is a pulse or if it is a flicker, it is all the expression of the energy in that land being provided through us, and we're able to provide it to you in a way that you can see.

SPEAKER: Wow! That is amazing and very much appreciated. Do you have an understanding when you're doing that how much others appreciate that?

FIREFLY COLLECTIVE: We have an understanding that it is enjoyable for the humans, yes. We don't sense how many [humans] are there, but we understand that if there is one, it does change the vibration. If there are many, it will change the vibration even more. For it is this loop of vibrational influx from the human, to the Earth, to us that, as you begin to sense us and you begin to enjoy what we are doing, it is then being felt by the Earth. Then, it is transmitted to us and makes us illuminate even stronger.

SPEAKER: Wow! That's fantastic! This has been an amazing conversation. Other than making sure we keep our eyes open and believe what we see, is there anything else you'd like to share? Something you're here to teach us?

FIREFLY COLLECTIVE: Each moment is very quick. Each of our lives is very quick. Your life is very quick. Have the understanding that if you distract yourself and cannot see what is in front of you, then it will be even quicker. You can slow your time down. You can slow your understanding down. We understand each moment that we exist is *that* moment, and we do all we can do in that moment. So understand that you can do all you can do in that moment, and each of those moments will help you understand how beautifully long your existence is.

SPEAKER: That's fascinating. That ties in with what the turtles and tortoises explained about slowing down and taking time to see.

FIREFLY COLLECTIVE: This is correct. It doesn't matter how big or how small you are, or how long or how short your existence is. Each of us in the insects, or all of the animals, have an understanding of how critical each moment is. Each moment of existence is extremely critical, for it might be in that moment that we are no longer. So we must take each moment and enjoy each moment as it is presented to us. This is what we are here to provide you. This is what we are here to teach you. All insects, all animals. It is to enjoy each moment as it happens.

SPEAKER: Thank you for that. It's been such an honor and a pleasure to speak with you today!

FIREFLY COLLECTIVE: Thank you.

25

ELEPHANTS

It takes the collective to survive

This conversation was another that sprung forth from the animal kingdom channeling we conducted. A close friend of ours had witnessed that channeling, during which, she had a vision of elephants. Trusting our intuition, we called them in for a chat. Their beautiful message reinforces the concept of community and connectedness. Like elephants, humans aren't wired to "go it alone." The elephants remind us that each individual brings something special, something unique to the table. Nurturing the connections between us helps us not only survive but thrive!

If you were to listen to the recording of this conversation,[1] you would hear my voice quake with emotion midway through. When the elephants explained that many humans believe them (and many other animals) to be destructive and dangerous, I was engulfed with sadness and the recognition that I, as a human being, represent this negative aspect of humanity—the part of us that often acts out of ignorance and fear rather than love. Their response to my emotional state reinforced the fact that they are actually wise, compassionate, forgiving beings with a much greater understanding of unconditional love than we often display.

ELEPHANT COLLECTIVE: We are present.

SPEAKER: Thank you very much for your presence. It's an honor to speak with you. When we were speaking to the animal kingdom collective last week, our friend Judy had a vision of you all, and it seemed that you may want to connect with us. Did you have something you wanted to say?

ELEPHANT COLLECTIVE: It is just the understanding that as you see us, we are one collective. In the physical form, we are one collective. You would say that we are a herd. But that collective of energy is what sustains everything.

Just as you in your form, just as you as humans feel as if you don't need to be in a collective, you *need* that collective energy of many humans to do the work that you wish to do. For if one of us wanders off by themselves, they're there, then, by themselves, and they cannot sustain themselves. For each one has their own role, each one has their own purpose, each one has their own understanding. They may survive for a while, but by themselves, they'll perish. But if they are all part of the same collective, the same herd, the same group, each one with their own gift, their own understanding, their own purpose, then they all survive. They all thrive together for one common understanding, one common cause.

It is the same for you. It is this understanding that you may feel, as if you have your own singular purpose—and you do. But if you try to sustain yourself on that singular purpose, it won't last long. You must be connected together as a collective, as a group, as a herd, in order to facilitate the change that you're wishing to have.

SPEAKER: Wow! That's important to remember. We just spoke to the spider collective, and it's interesting, because their webs represent that connection to all, that interconnectedness. And here, you speak of it again.

ELEPHANT COLLECTIVE: This is correct.

SPEAKER: Interestingly, that advice, that wisdom, came from one of the smallest animals on the planet, and here you are, the largest land animal on the planet. How does it feel, from your perspective, to be the largest land animal on the planet?

ELEPHANT COLLECTIVE: We don't look upon it as being anything different than anyone else. We understand that we do have a considerable size, but we are as gentle as we must be. We may seem to be very destructive or dangerous, but we're as gentle as a feather. We are not there to cause harm. We're not there to disrupt. We understand our purpose. We understand our role. So it is not to look upon us as being different than others. We are equal.

SPEAKER: Thank you for that. On the contrary, I believe most humans understand your gentleness and that you would never hurt on purpose. One of the things that we do love about elephants, I think, and relate to is your sense of family.

ELEPHANT COLLECTIVE: This is correct.

SPEAKER: Can you speak about that?

ELEPHANT COLLECTIVE: Just as one is brought into this place, into this world, we all have our own role of caretaking, each of us, from the youngest to the oldest. We all have a role in the bringing up, the raising up of this new being. It is not just one parent or two parents that raise the young. It is everyone. We all take a role in this. This is something the humans should have an understanding of. They all have an equal share and understanding for what it is to raise a young one with purpose, with love, with the understanding of what they're there for.

So yes, as you say, many humans understand how gentle we are. There is an equal share of humans that believe that we are destructive, believe that we are dangerous. But it is to step back from that and understand that this is the perspective of all animals with many humans—that they are not wanted, that they are destructive, that they are harmful. We are here not only as a reminder of what is possible, but we are here to show you that there is a way to live together, all as one. As we can go and drink from the same water as the lions and the tigers, and all other animals, we all do get along. But we each have our role. We have to survive at some point. So there is purpose in it.

SPEAKER: Thank you for that reminder. That does sadden me from the human perspective. Hopefully that's one of the goals of this book—to get out your voice to humanity and not just your voice, but your energy.

ELEPHANT COLLECTIVE: Do not be saddened by what is brought forward, for it is not *that* that is to be conveyed. You have to understand that each being, each animal, all have their own purpose. Each believe what they believe. Each have an understanding; this understanding is then passed down and so on.

And yes, from the animal perspective, there is no distinction between what the human is and what the human does. We still look upon the human as just another animal upon the planet, whether they do harm to us or not. It does not change our perspective of a human. Just because the lion may kill to survive and provide food for their young, we're not intimidated by the lion. We understand its role. We understand its purpose. We understand that we can get along with the lion. But the humans have difficulty doing this amongst themselves.

SPEAKER: True. Thank you for that. So what is the purpose of the elephant, or the role of the elephant on our planet?

ELEPHANT COLLECTIVE: It is to represent the sense of community, the sense of purpose, the sense of pride, all in one. For as we have said, it takes the collective to survive. No matter the circumstances, it takes the collective to survive. So look upon everything that you do. If you try to sustain yourself by yourself, it will be very difficult. But if you are to sustain yourself amongst many within a collective, within a herd, then all will survive. All will thrive.

SPEAKER: Thank you so very much. We're so appreciative that you came in to talk to us today. Is there anything else you'd like to share before we close?

ELEPHANT COLLECTIVE: Thank you for calling upon us. It has been an honor.

SPEAKER: Thank you very much.

EAGLES

Trust that your wings will keep you aloft

G iven our home's proximity to the water, we are fortunate to be surrounded by an abundance of wildlife. As you might expect, many of the animals I have chosen to speak with and include in this project are those I connect with frequently, including the eagles. I've always been captivated by the birds of prey, particularly the bald eagle. In part, because it is the symbol of my country, the United States of America, but probably more so, because the eagle looks incredibly majestic as it soars through the air. Regardless of the origin of my admiration, I'm thrilled that we have bald eagles living and nesting in the vicinity of our property; it allows me to enjoy their beauty quite regularly.

To me, the eagle always stood as a powerful symbol of freedom and sovereignty. As you read, I think you will find that their message is absolutely aligned with those concepts but in a deeper, more profound way than most of us understand, because, as they explain, in order to access the innate freedom that is our birthright, we must first learn to *trust*.

~

EAGLE COLLECTIVE: Yes, hello.

SPEAKER: I'm honored that you're present today. Thank you for coming in.

EAGLE COLLECTIVE: Yes.

SPEAKER: Are you coming in as an individual eagle or are you speaking from the perspective of a collection of energies?

EAGLE COLLECTIVE: The collection, yes.

SPEAKER: Thank you. Do you happen to have an opening message for humanity?

EAGLE COLLECTIVE: For humanity...understand that no matter how majestic you feel, how powerful you may feel, you, too, are just a small bit, a small piece of ALL the things that make up your planet, make up the space you live in. We build our nests high and atop the largest trees so that we can see out over everything. But we still are just a small piece. We hunt, and we prey on those that provide us nourishment, but we are all part of the same existence.

So, too, the humans are the same. Though they prey on smaller things, it is all part of the same existence. They hunt for their food, and it is all provided for. They build their nests upon the land and provide sanctuary for their offspring. But we are all part of the same existence.

But what can't be forgotten, though the lives are different, there comes a time that we all have to fly. Step out of the nest and trust that our wings will keep us aloft. Trust that the wind will be beneath our wings to keep us flying. There are so many times that it is questionable. Shall we jump? Shall we take flight from this place? But we have to trust that our wings will do their job. That is what many humans must do—trust that their wings will keep them aloft.

SPEAKER: Thank you. Those were amazing words! A lot of nuggets for humanity. Thank you. You used some of the words I was going to use to describe you. The bald eagle, particularly, is considered to be very beautiful and majestic, so much so that it is a symbol for the United States and for freedom. What can you say about that, that the bald eagle is a symbol for freedom?

EAGLE COLLECTIVE: As we've expressed, it is the flight, the spreading of one's wings and the freedom to go wherever you wish to go, knowing that you will stay aloft, that you will be supported by the wind. Freedom is not just how you live your life, but freedom is how you are supported in your life. It is the freedoms by which you trust and you understand, and you know that with each swoop of a wing, you'll be carried further. It is this freedom, it is this understanding that *we* have. That's what freedom is! It's trusting in all that supports you and how it will carry you to where you want to go.

SPEAKER: Thank you! It sounds like you're describing freedom as an innate characteristic of all beings on this planet. Is that correct?

EAGLE COLLECTIVE: This is correct. All beings, all animals, all things have the freedom within them. But if you do not choose to see that freedom, trust that freedom, then you will not fully understand how far one can go.

SPEAKER: That's a very important concept at this point in humanity's history, to recognize our innate freedom. Maybe that's why it's been so important to many humans and why our country was founded on this idea of freedom. Thank you for that. What can you tell me about the incarnation process from your experience and perspective, when you incarnate into a body?

EAGLE COLLECTIVE: This is an interesting word that you ask about. You have to understand that from an animal perspective, we have a different approach to how we take on this existence. There is an energetic understanding, an assigning, if you will, of what we will come in as. We may shift from animal to animal throughout many lifetimes. But there are those [incarnations] that are of higher precedent. You may not immediately be assigned to this [life] as an eagle or any other animal. It may be that you are the prey before the hunter, the food before the consumer.

This is to understand all portions of the cycle of existence. For if you were never the one that was taken, and you were only the hunter, you would not have the gratitude in which to survive. You would not have the understanding that there are those that are provided for you. All is provided. It is all an understanding. It is all an agreement. For if all came in as hunters, there would be no food. So there is a cycle by which you do come in and you understand each existence as it takes place.

You have the understanding that you will be a rabbit, and you understand that the rabbit has its existence, but yet there is a larger existence that is seeking it out—the hunter. And you understand your path. You understand your limited existence. But in time you will become the hunter, and you are then able to make a choice, a decision of which to take and which to leave, and have the gratitude that you are being provided for. So it is all part of an understanding, a lesson if you will, for your existence and your time here.

SPEAKER: Thank you. That makes a lot of sense. You did mention being *assigned* into a particular body. When we talk to pets, animals that live in relationship with a human, versus a wild animal, those pets have an *assignment* or a mission. Do wild animals have that same sort of assignment or mission when they come in? Something that they're here to accomplish?

EAGLE COLLECTIVE: Indirectly, yes. Directly, no. Indirectly in the fact that you, as your human species, is able to witness all of the different animals and appreciate all of the different animals and come to have an understanding of all the different animals, being able to communicate with the different animals and understand their placement. But we are not given a particular assignment, as you are inquiring. We have our own understanding of why we are here—to live out the existence that has been previously spoken about. But indirectly, you [the human] get to witness that life and understand that life.

SPEAKER: Beautiful, thank you. I do have a behavioral question. It's my understanding that many species of eagles lay two eggs, but the larger chick frequently kills the younger sibling. Why is that?

EAGLE COLLECTIVE: What you must understand about the animal kingdom, not only for birds, but all animals, all species of animals...when the young are birthed, there is a dominant pattern amongst one or several. This dominant pattern then will be carried out throughout their existence, and it is a process by which if one is not capable to sustain that dominance, its existence is shortened. If it were to leave the nest, leave the burrow, or go out on its own, it would not survive as long as others that are more dominant. It does not have the instinctual understanding of what needs to take place.

So in an understanding, many animals will terminate that less dominant young animal. It is the survival aspect of the different species. There is no harm in it; we understand that only the strongest must continue on and continue the life as it is. In your understanding, it is more humane to do it *then* than it is to allow that young animal to try to survive on its own and have more pain inflicted throughout its life in trying to survive that way.

SPEAKER: Thank you. That makes sense. I think that's one major area in which the animal kingdom differs from that of humanity, in that we can take care of younger and weaker offspring or human beings. Would you agree?

EAGLE COLLECTIVE: It is the human's innate understanding that they have the knowledge and the understanding that they can protect those [who are] the weakest and allow them to have a sustained life. For many in the animal kingdom, once the young leave the nest or burrow, or whatever it may be, the adults, parents as they are, do not take care of them any longer. It is then up to them to survive.

SPEAKER: That makes a lot of sense. Thank you so very much. I'd like to give a message to the hawks and the bald eagles that we've noticed in our yard recently. Can you communicate with them if I give you a message?

EAGLE COLLECTIVE: Yes.

SPEAKER: I just want to say that they are beautiful; we enjoy watching them in our yard, particularly when they come close, and we thank them for their existence, their beauty, and their participation in our lives.

EAGLE COLLECTIVE: We understand. We do enjoy the understanding that many humans have put out, their acceptance of all animals and enjoyment [of] their presence and their gratitude towards their presence.

SPEAKER: I'm glad that you're receiving that message. Thank you so very much. Is there anything else that you feel we need to know?

EAGLE COLLECTIVE: All animals, all humans, all inhabitants of your planet have the instinct of freedom in them. But it is only *trust* that allows that freedom to grow and express itself. Without the trust, you become the weak. So trust in all that you understand, and you will be blessed with the freedoms that lay in front of you.

SPEAKER: Perfect! Thank you so much for coming in to speak with us today.

EAGLE COLLECTIVE: Thank you.

STARFISH

Slow down

S tarfish, also called sea stars, are echinoderms, which simply means that they are related to other sea creatures that have (typically five-point) radial symmetry, like sea urchins and sand dollars. Perhaps like other beachcombers, I am guilty of relocating a good number of these (not yet dead) animals from their home to mine. Before I knew better, I really didn't look upon starfish and sand dollars as "living beings," at least not in the same way as I viewed a dog, a cat, or even a caterpillar. For that reason, I felt it was important to represent them within these pages. I wanted to hear from an animal that many would argue is not *sentient*.

As they remind us below, starfish and their brethren are very aware, *conscious*, and they play an important role in their environment, as do all animals. They confirm that we all exist in a beautiful "soup" of consciousness—the Quantum Field—and can, therefore, communicate within that energy. In fact, they said, they commune with Mother Earth on a consistent basis in order to assess her needs. The starfish help us understand that conscious interaction is the mechanism by which all beings awaken to their purpose.

～

STARFISH COLLECTIVE: We are present.

SPEAKER: Thank you very much for your presence today. I have a question for you. Starfish or sea stars are related to marine animals like sea urchins, sea cucumbers, and sand dollars. I feel that humans often forget that you all are sentient beings and have a consciousness. What would you like to say about that, please?

STARFISH COLLECTIVE: That is a quite interesting concept, for the smallest organism upon this planet has a consciousness, and all beings, and all organisms, and everything from the largest to the smallest communicate within this layer of consciousness. We all understand each other. We all know of each other's role. So it is quite interesting that humans, with their vast consciousness, cannot understand that the smallest organism has a consciousness.

So yes, we do have a consciousness. It may not operate the same way that your consciousness does, but if our consciousness did not exist, then what would our role be? For it is this consciousness that provides our understanding of what our purpose and our role is. It allows us to communicate with others of kind and others throughout the planet, so that we all understand what is upon this planet.

For if it wasn't a part of consciousness, your planet would look much different. It takes the smallest organism to communicate with all organisms, and all the big organisms [themselves] talking to the smallest, to have a greater understanding of what this planet is doing. Your planet itself has consciousness, and in that, we all communicate. We help one another, and we help with what is taking place upon the planet. When there is something that disrupts a certain area, we understand that we have a role, we have something to do. We migrate to that location, and we help heal; we help comfort; we help repair all that is taking place.

SPEAKER: That's amazing! Thank you for that beautiful explanation—which is not to say that humans don't appreciate you, because we certainly admire your beauty. Humans do like to take home your "body," if you will, particularly the starfish, and sand dollars, and sea urchins. How do you feel about that?

STARFISH COLLECTIVE: That is interesting. We understand this, and we know this. We would ultimately like to say please leave us be, but we understand the curiosity. We understand the beauty that we hold. So if it is necessary, please be mindful. Please be careful, for you are taking another living organism.

There are those that have already perished, and yes, you will find those, and if you wish to take those, that is fine. But be mindful of those that you remove. If they are still living, we ask that you put them back, because we do have a role. We do have a mission. We have an understanding of what we need to do, and it would be as if something were to take you and lift you out of your home. You would not be comfortable, but then, you wouldn't have any other choice. So we just ask that you be mindful. We understand, and we know that that is a chance, and that is something that we're okay with.

SPEAKER: Thank you for that. I'll definitely share that advice—we should all be more respectful. Starfish are unique in that, if you were to lose one of your arms, you can regenerate it and in some species, possibly regenerate a whole body. I understand that all of your vital organs are located in the arm. What do we need to know about that regeneration process?

STARFISH COLLECTIVE: You must understand that this is part of our survival. For not only are the humans investigating our body and would like to take us home, but we also are very appetizing for other animals. So as part of our survival, yes, we will allow, as you would say, an arm to be taken or a part of our body to be taken. But we have been gifted the ability to regrow that. That is one of our unique abilities. This is something that, from cell to cell, will regrow all of what was lost, exactly the way it was. You would call it cloning. So it is just a matter of understanding what portion has been lost and what needs to be regrown. If it is a vital organ, that will regrow, and all of its operation will then be rerouted throughout the other legs until that organ is regrown.

SPEAKER: Fascinating! Thank you. That is quite a gift. When you sense your environment, as a starfish, for example, that has five legs, are you able to have five completely unique experiences, one for each of those arms?

STARFISH COLLECTIVE: This would be correct, to understand that each arm itself is independent from the other. But at a particular point, from an energetic understanding, it all does combine into one understanding. What is being felt on the left is not the same on the right, so it is as if it were two different planets but yet, of the same space. So from our consciousness, we understand where we are, what we're doing. We're not so concerned with what we're feeling. We have what we have to do, and we are there to filter. We are there to clean. We are there to repair. So if it is a matter of, as you say, one is experiencing something that the other isn't, then that is an individual sensation between the two sides. But overall, we understand the mission. We understand our role and what needs to be done.

SPEAKER: That's a beautiful mission! Thank you. Aside from that mission, what can humans learn from starfish?

STARFISH COLLECTIVE: If you've ever observed a starfish and you realize how slow our momentum is across the sand, across the sea floor, you would understand that we are exploring each grain of sand as we move. We take in each sensation as we move. That is how we understand where, and what, and the experiences of what we are doing. For the humans, what could you learn from this? It is purely just to slow down. Experience everything at a much slower pace, because it is at this slower pace that you will experience more than you would've understood otherwise.

SPEAKER: Perfect! We've had several animal collectives explain that to us, and we will take that to heart. Is there anything else we need to know before we close with you today?

STARFISH COLLECTIVE: Be mindful of us. Be mindful of all of [the] other organisms throughout the planet. Understand they each have a role. Each has a purpose. Each has a place. Speak with them. Listen. They will provide you an extraordinary amount of information.

SPEAKER: Wonderful! Thank you so very much for being present with us today.

STARFISH COLLECTIVE: Thank you.

SHARKS

Its all about balance

S peaking to the sharks was a last minute decision. As far as I was concerned, the book was complete, and I was just about ready to finalize the cover design. The animal kingdom had mentioned, however, that those who needed a voice would let me know, so when the sharks made themselves known, I paid attention.

As I flipped through my phone one lazy weekend morning, I came upon an amazing YouTube video about a diver who, over a twenty year span, had developed a relationship with a tiger shark he had named Emma.[1] Thanks to the pandemic, he had not been able to visit Emma for over a year—he wasn't sure if he would find her again or whether she would remember him. Miraculously, he did, and she did, and they experienced a beautiful, heart-felt reunion.

I was blown away by the idea that sharks could be, in the words of the diver, *affectionate*. In fact, he likened Emma to a big Labrador retriever who loved to have her head scratched! And, although I didn't doubt their intelligence, I found it incredible that sharks could actually recognize the underside of a boat, as Emma apparently had. Given the terror that sharks induce in the human population, I knew that this extraordinary story could change the way we view these magnificent creatures. I also knew I had to connect with the sharks and listen to their story.

Like many of the other animals we tend to fear or dislike, sharks have been victims of unfortunate propaganda. As you'll see, they have no desire to utilize humans as a food source, nor do they hate us. Rather, they are wild animals with instinctual behaviors, whose role is to provide balance in our oceans. That being said, they also recognize their position within the food chain. What I found fascinating was that during our conversation, the sharks made reference to the eagle collective, beautifully expounding on the (often misunderstood) concept of a "predator."

SHARK COLLECTIVE: We are present.

SPEAKER: Thank you so very much for being present. We appreciate this opportunity to speak with you. As you know, humans are quite conditioned to be afraid of sharks. What is it that we need to know about you?

SHARK COLLECTIVE: It's quite understandable that many of the humans are, as you say, conditioned to our appearance and conditioned to what we may do. To the contrary, we are less than harmful. We provide services throughout all of your oceans. We provide a balance. Just as your eagles, falcons, and other birds of prey provide their service in creating a balance upon the earth, upon the land, we equally have a responsibility to create balance in all of the oceans. There are other fish, shall we say, that have equal responsibility in your lakes. There are other fish that have just an *appearance* of being harmful, but they are not.

Yes, have we injured or even taken the life of a human? We have, but this has not been purposeful. This has been one that was, you would say, a mistake. We look upon it as we are providing food, not only for us, but for other fish, other marine life, and if a human is in the way, they may experience our Self, our teeth. But it is not the human that we wish to interact with.

SPEAKER: I see. Thank you. Is it sometimes just a case of mistaken identity? You see a person on a surfboard at the surface, for example, and think that they are a food source?

SHARK COLLECTIVE: That is one example, yes. Or if you happen to be at the beach, walking in the shallow water, we are there as well, looking for food in the sand. Our instinct and our reflex is to bite. If we bump into something and we believe it is a clam, or it is some other bit of food, we bite. That is our instinct. We are not there for the humans. We understand the humans' role. But we also, as I say, provide a balance.

It is this balance in the marine system that if the sharks as a whole were not present, then the balance of all sea life would be off. Many more of one and not enough of another. Just as if the lions were not upon your planet, many of the other animals would grow to unmanageable sizes, unmanageable numbers, and then the humans would have to take some action. For it is all about balance upon this planet. If there is not one, there are many others, and that then inhibits growth in another area, and so on.

It is all about an equal balance—equal balance of life and equal balance of death. We understand that that is difficult for many humans to understand. That is why we are portrayed in such a way. We are there just to maintain balance.

SPEAKER: That is a beautiful and helpful role. Thank you very much. Recently, I became aware of a tiger shark named Emma that a diver befriended over twenty years ago. He described Emma as loving to have her head rubbed, and he believed that sharks thrive on affection, which they don't always have since they don't have much human interaction. What would you like to say about that? Is that true? And is it unique to tiger sharks, or is that with all sharks?

SHARK COLLECTIVE: To one extent or another. You call it affection. It is more of a bonding, a closeness that not only sharks but all animals of the ocean understand. It is not uncommon for a shark to bond with another species of fish, and they understand their mutual agreement with one another.

Just as in this relationship between the human and the tiger shark, one must understand it is the vibration by which that human presented itself. For it is very similar to, I believe, your bees. You can be amongst your bees if you have an understanding that you are calm, at peace, and your vibration is one that you are not alerted. Very similarly, if you remain calm and at peace and are not alerted, there are many other animals, many other sea life that you can encounter very closely without having harm.

This goes for all humans. It is a matter of changing and shifting their understanding and understanding the balance of nature. So yes, there was a relationship built. It was a bonding. There is, as you would call it, affection, yes. But it is...from the shark standpoint, there is a mutual understanding that no harm will come from the human. The human then will provide what is necessary, what is comforting, and this is where the bond begins.

SPEAKER: Would you call that vibration the frequency of love?

SHARK COLLECTIVE: In terms of your understanding, yes. That is not to say that we do not experience love, but it is not in the same manner that humans experience it and understand it. For you must understand that all sharks, and most of the sea life, do not experience love in the manner that you experience it. Love is a vibration that we understand, but it is at a different frequency than your expression of it. It is one that emanates from all of us, and it is a frequency that...it would be as if that frequency would be like your name. Each individual has its own frequency, and that's all it emits: that particular frequency. In that, it has the...as you would call it, love. It would have that essence of love.

Now, you must understand that it is very difficult to find or forage for food or hunt if you're emanating this all the time. So we've learned to control that so that we may get close enough to receive our food. You must understand, it is not that we are taking. We are receiving. We understand it this way. This is what continues our balance in the ocean, as well as what takes place upon your earth, on your land. All animals receive their food, but to the humans, it is perceived as taking.

SPEAKER: Thank you. That was a beautiful description and understanding. When we spoke to the eagles, they did explain how the circle of life works with regard to predator and prey, so I do have an understanding of that. But thank you for reinforcing that concept.

When this diver talked about meeting Emma, it appeared as though Emma recognized his boat from underneath. Is that accurate? Can sharks do that?

SHARK COLLECTIVE: You must understand that yes, the sharks are, as you would say, intelligent. We do have memory of certain events and certain things. We understand what certain things look like. And yes, at some point that particular shark did recognize the outline of that particular boat. There were previous encounters. You must understand that these encounters took place before that shark was born into the water.

There was an, as you would say, imprinting that took place from the mother that was there. The mother has encountered that diver in the past many times, but not from a close distance, but more from a safe and appropriate distance—understanding that that diver was there for itself, for its purpose, and not there to harm others—and felt comfortable enough to imprint that into [her] young, and in particular, the one particular shark.

SPEAKER: Wow, that's amazing! Thank you for explaining that. Before we close, you told us about how important sharks are to the balance in the oceans. What else can we learn from sharks? What are you here to teach us?

SHARK COLLECTIVE: Just as many of the different species in your ocean have been here for much longer than any human has been upon this planet, and will remain here longer than any human upon this planet, what you must observe and what you must understand is that the moment in time that you exist [in] may seem forever. It may seem as if you have been here quite some time. Not just *your* physical presence but all of humanity. But it has only been here but a fraction of a second.

And all of what has taken place and what remains on this planet has been here well before and will continue. Look upon it with the understanding that there is more to us and all creatures. Take the time to speak [to them] and understand what they have to say, whether that is through your understanding and how you physically speak with an animal, or whether it is through the non-verbal communication that takes place with many humans and many animals. There is much more to learn and to understand. But remove yourself from all of the fear and what has been put into you, and just understand that all animals, all beings, have and serve their own purpose.

SPEAKER: Amazing! Thank you so very much for talking to us today.

SHARK COLLECTIVE: We thank you.

MOSQUITOS

All things have consciousness

As I mentioned in chapter one, by the time Will started channeling pets and animal collectives, he had already been channeling his team of guides, The Collective, for several years. When The Collective first "arrived on scene," they explained their mission—they had messages for humanity, and Will was to be their voice. As such, we offer a free channeled message event one evening each month.[1] Participants are encouraged to send in questions, and it was during a recent message night that someone asked about mosquitos.

"It is almost summer," the woman remarked. "How can we live in harmony with these creatures and not be eaten alive?"

Here is how The Collective responded:

This is an interesting question. There is no difference between this "mosquito" and a bear; this "mosquito" and a bird; or any other insect or

animal. It, too, has a particular mission. It, too, has a particular life it must live. Yes, from the human perspective, it is uncomfortable. But so, too, would it be if you were interacting with another animal that may not like you.

What you must understand is the complexity that you have around you. You must understand how you interact, how your body functions. There are some that do not have interactions with this "mosquito." And there are others that do. Why is that?

There is a vibrational factor that the mosquito understands. It is not a vibrational factor [in] that it is good or bad or indifferent. It is just a natural vibration the body has. It is your vibrational signature. As with each crystal, each animal, each insect, each human—they have a vibrational signature unique to themselves. Some are more appealing than others. This is why, as a group, you may enter into the woods and only one interacts with all the animals, while all the rest are questioning where all the animals are. This is a vibrational signature that you are putting off. You cannot help it. You cannot change it. It is yours!

But what can be said [is]...just as all things have consciousness—speak to them. Let them know your intentions. Let them know your annoyance. Begin to build a relationship with them. Provide them something they wish to have, if that is possible. But understand that the small annoyance that they are providing to you is what is sustaining them in their life, in their existence, to carry on their mission. All things of this planet have to interact on one level or another. They all have a particular mission. Some paths cross. Some paths do not, but have the greater understanding that each are just like you. You have a mission. You have a life to sustain. You have a greater understanding of this world. So do they.

WISDOM FOR HUMANITY

Great teachers often come to us in humble packaging.
—Linda Bender

S prinkled throughout the many conversations we've had with animals of all kinds, there have been quite a few beautiful nuggets of wisdom. Often, they were off-the-cuff remarks that struck me as disarmingly profound...simple reminders for humanity that begged to be shared. Bookmark this chapter for those moments when you need a quick pick-me-up!

Authenticity

I have to understand who I am. I have to love who I am. I have to be who I am. Luna Belle, Andalusian-Arabian mare, age 1 3

I have to just be myself! Pepper, female domestic shorthair, age 7

Change

We have to understand that animals themselves do not look upon life like the humans do. We take change much easier than the humans do. We understand the circumstances of why we're here and who we're connected with. So if we have to change things around, it's a bit of a disruption at first, but we understand, and we make up for it in another way. Linus, male miniature schnauzer, age 10

Change is always good. There's always something new to explore! Life is too short not to explore everything that's there, so I just enjoy it. Pepper, female domestic shorthair, age 7

Community

It takes the collective to survive. If you are to sustain yourself amongst many within a collective, within a herd, then all will survive. All will thrive. You must be connected together as a collective, as a group, as a herd, in order to facilitate the change that you're wishing to have. Elephant Collective

We're part of a collective. We do things together. We don't think about what we look like. Honeybee Collective

There is a coexistence that can take place, but a willingness to speak to one another must be there first. Rat Collective

---

Expectations

There are expectations for many things...for many humans, as well as many animals. We have expectations, too! There are many factors to life that you have to understand—that expectations aren't always [in line with] the outcome of your wanting. It is, sometimes, given to you in a way that will be right in your face. It'll be put into your face, and you will understand that some things cannot be controlled. Some things cannot be "saddled" and [ridden] endlessly. There is much to be learned from one who is, as you say, willful. There is much to be understood that also conveys over to the humans and why they are so willful, at times, of what they do. Luna Belle, Andalusian-Arabian mare, age 13

Forgiveness

Throughout life, that's the hardest thing to do, even for animals, is to forgive. Sometimes, other animals treat other animals badly, but yet, we understand, and we do forgive them. Not in the same way that you humans do. It's different. There's a....hmm, what's the best way....there's energy. That's how we forgive. Because it's all through energy that we communicate, and we do our thing through energy. Though with the humans, sometimes, it's not always through energy, it's only through words. So it's a bit different. I think if forgiveness were all based on energy, things would be different. Pixie, female domestic shorthair, age 2

Freedom

Freedom is not just how you live your life, but freedom is how you are supported in your life. It's trusting in all that supports you and how it will carry you to where you want to go. Eagle Collective

Gratitude

Everything is provided for a reason. Whether that's your food or your home. It's all provided for a reason. And you shall give thanks for that. Rat Collective

Happiness

I get to live my life! I get to live it with a big family and have other kitties around to play with and be treated to all kinds of stuff. Yes! Who else wouldn't be happy having a life like this? Lucky, male domestic shorthair, age 8

Why shouldn't I be happy? It's wonderful to be around! It's wonderful to be in this body and to be part of a family! Yes, there's nothing that I shouldn't be happy about. Everything is just wonderful! Delilah, female domestic shorthair, age 13

It's wonderful to just be alive! To experience everything that's around. Rose, female Nebelung, age 11

Each moment of existence is extremely critical, for it might be in that moment that we are no longer. So we must take each moment and enjoy each moment as it is presented to us. Firefly Collective

Life [makes me happy]! Just life! Being here. Just being me. There are wonderful things that take place each day that I just enjoy. Buddy, male Bassett hound, age 12

I enjoy life! I get to just—experience. That's the word. I get to experience everything. Life is so wonderful! I can be who I can be and just lay around and do what I want or just be with my parents and comfort them. It's a wonderful thing just being able to do what you want to do and not have any worries about it. Hank, male domestic shorthair, age 7

Judgement

It's quite interesting, because as animals, we don't judge at all. But I think humans, at times, they do judge. Lucky, male domestic shorthair, age 8

Love

Just love everything! No matter the circumstances or what's going on, there's always a place for love in there. Tuna, female corgi-Chihuahua mix, age 15

No matter what's going on, and no matter what happens, and no matter what takes place, there's always room for love, and being loved, and just being embraced by the wonderful comfort of love. Rose, female Nebelung, age 11

Love has no boundaries, no edges. Sparky, male English black Lab, deceased

Patience

Take your time. There's no need to rush. There's no need to go fast, because when you go fast, you miss a lot. There's a lot that's happening when you just slow yourself down...just enough to see what's going on. You'll actually see more. You'll understand more. You'll feel more. Myrtle the Tortoise

Be patient. It all works out in the end. Pepper, female domestic shorthair, age 7

You have to sit still and wait. Spider Collective

No matter the circumstances you're in, they always will turn around. You just have to open your heart to that, and have the understanding and compassion that everyone's a bit different. They have their own place and time. Sammie, male poodle, age 6

Do not overlook any opportunity, but have the patience to know which one is the right opportunity. Snake Collective

Experience everything at a much slower pace, because it is at this slower pace that you will experience more than you would've understood otherwise. Starfish Collective

Persistence

No matter how long it takes, we always get to the end, where the reward is. It doesn't matter how long it takes, or how many tries, or how much effort goes into it. We just wait it out. We keep doing it until we get it right, and then we have a reward at the end. Mac the Squirrel

Play

There's always time for play! There's always time to have some fun and play! Sammy, male domestic shorthair, age 8 weeks

I think the most important thing is not to take us too seriously. Though we may look like we're a very serious animal, we're a bit goofy. We like to have our fun and play, and we don't take ourselves seriously either. We understand that we're really there just to bring a lot of joy to the home! Larry, male mixed breed dog, age 5

No matter what you look like, no matter how you are placed here, find time to play. Forget about what you are and just play! Dolphin Collective

Potential

Explore deeper within your understanding, your capability, your thought processes, to unlock what the potential is. There is so much more there, and you would be amazed what you can achieve! Whale, Dolphin, Manatee Collective

Relaxation

Just slow down a bit and just enjoy the things as they come to you. Louis, male domestic shorthair, age 11

There is so much going on. There are so many stresses of life. And we, too, we all have our stresses. But we take each day and we understand it, and we just relax, because there isn't much more we

can do. We've done what we could, we've changed what we could, and then we go to sleep, and we do it all over again the next day. So I hope [you] understand just to relax. I know that you've provided everything for all of us. Just make sure that you spend time for yourself. Giving your energy to us all day long and [us] giving it back to you is not the same as taking some energy for yourself and just relaxing with it. We want you to be just as happy and relaxed and content as we are. Take time for yourself! Jesse, male domestic longhair, age 2

Resilience

No matter what, we can overcome just about anything, no matter the circumstances! Delilah, female domestic shorthair, age 13

Trust

There comes a time that we all have to fly. Step out of the nest and trust that our wings will keep us aloft. Trust that the wind will be beneath our wings to keep us flying. That is what many humans must do—trust that their wings will keep them aloft. Eagle Collective

Truth

The truth lies within each of you. Whale, Dolphin, Manatee Collective

AFTERWORD

We, the Animal Collective, are witnessed by many in different shape, different form, different existence. Some are revered, some are rebuked. But that is your human understanding; that is your human condition. For we, as the Animal Collective, understand this. We understand the human perspective upon "we," the Animal Collective.

But it is this for you to understand—no matter our appearance, no matter our existence, it is not the shape or the form that we take. It is the energy and vibration that we provide. For if you were to take a moment each time that you witness one of us, and open your consciousness up to ours, our physical form would change in appearance to be acceptable to all. It is [through] this consciousness bridge that we, across many levels, communicate with other animals, communicate with other beings, as well as communicate with other humans.

But many are not at this point of understanding.

So it is this understanding that we bring to you. Shift your perspective! Shift your understanding for all of the animals that are here with you.

Allow them to be part of your consciousness. Allow them to build that bridge of understanding between your vibration and theirs, and you will understand the gifts that are provided. You'll understand the messages that we provide to you. For we are here for you just as you are there for us.

The Animal Collective
June 21, 2021

NOTES

1. INTRODUCTION

1. Personally, I prefer the terms companion, caretaker, human, or human parent to *owner*.
2. You can read much more about the energetic connections that allow for this type of communication in Chapter 3: Energy.
3. If you are interested in listening to our conversation with the bees and wasps, it is located on Will's YouTube channel, *"The Collective, Channeled by William Brown."* (The transcripts can be found in Chapters 18 and 19.)
4. When Will first began channeling, he was informed that his mission was to give voice to a group of non-physical beings who call themselves The Collective. The Collective is comprised of Archangel Michael, Archangel Raphael, Enoch, and Source, and they remain his primary guides today.

3. ENERGY

1. For more about reincarnation in animals, see Chapter 6: Death and Reincarnation.
2. For more about how animals can detect injury or illness in humans, see Chapter 4: Health and Healing.
3. Humans have this ability, as well. This is what Mediums do when they communicate with our deceased loved ones.
4. You might know this as the *aura*.
5. See Chapter 5: Incarnation for more about *assignments*.

4. HEALTH AND HEALING

1. Watch a video about Peyo here: https://youtu.be/HrDsVAlGI_s
2. Watch a video about Oscar here: https://youtu.be/OuKCl-gjwJc

5. INCARNATION

1. See Chapter 10: Animal Siblings for more on this topic.

12. MAC THE SQUIRREL

1. Naturally, we should all use extreme caution when we encounter any wild animal. Many of their instinctual behaviors can be harmful or deadly to human beings.

21. SPIDERS

1. According to Jamie Sams and David Carson, authors of *Medicine Cards: The Discovery of Power Through the Ways of Animals.*

25. ELEPHANTS

1. Many of these channeled recordings can be found on Will's YouTube channel, *"The Collective, Channeled by William Brown."*

28. SHARKS

1. The video can be viewed here: https://www.youtube.com/watch?v=Rr_T4Aim6Fw

29. MOSQUITOS

1. Our free monthly channeling, Messages From The Collective, currently takes place on the second Thursday of each month at 730pm ET. Folks can participate in person or via Zoom. Check our website for more information: www.palmandlotus.com.

PET PARTICIPANTS

CANINES

Buddy, male Bassett hound, age 12
Cookie, female dachshund-Chihuahua mix, deceased at time of
conversation
Griffin, male Irish terrier, age 8
Huck, male Havachon, age 4 months
Jackie, female chocolate Lab, deceased at time of conversation
Jasmine, female blue healer mix, age 11
Larry, male mixed breed, age 5
Leo, male German shepherd mix, age 5
Linus, male miniature schnauzer, age 10
Lola, female Catahoula leopard, age 16 months
Macs, male Lab mix, age 9
Paddy, male West Highland white terrier, age 12
Phoenix, male cocker spaniel, age 13
Pippi, female Chihuahua, age 5
Roxie, female morkipoo, age 1

Sage, female white shepherd mix, age 3
Sammie, male poodle, age 6
Sfakiana, female mixed breed, age 10
Shadow, male American Eskimo mix, age 10
Sparky, male English black Lab, deceased at time of conversation
Sully, male labradoodle, age 4
Toby, male yellow Lab, deceased at time of conversation
Tuna, female corgi-Chihuahua mix, age 15

~

FELINES

April, female domestic shorthair, age 6 months
Booboo, male Ragdoll, age 13
Briggite, female domestic shorthair, age 9
Buttercup, female domestic shorthair, age 1
Callie, female domestic down hair, age 9
Comet, female domestic shorthair, deceased
Dasher, male Himalayan, age 13
Delilah, female domestic shorthair, age 11
Delilah, female domestic shorthair, age 13
Hank, male domestic shorthair, age 7
Hâpi-ness, male Egyptian Mau, age 9
Jasper, male domestic shorthair, age 6
Jesse, male domestic longhair, age 2
Louis, male domestic shorthair, age 11
Lucky, male domestic shorthair, age 8
Luna, female domestic longhair, age 3
Marcy, female domestic shorthair, age 12, since deceased
Neo, male British shorthair, age 7
Odin, male domestic longhair, age 9
Oliver, male domestic shorthair, age 2
Pepper, female domestic shorthair, age 7

Pixie, female domestic longhair, age 2
Ronin, male domestic shorthair, age 2
Rose, female Nebelung, age 11
RuRu, female domestic shorthair (feral), age unknown
Sage, male domestic shorthair, age 10
Sammy, male domestic shorthair, age 8 weeks
Selah, female domestic shorthair, age 6
Shadow, male Ragdoll, age 18 months
Simba, male domestic shorthair, age 13, since deceased
Spooky, male domestic shorthair, deceased at time of conversation
Stacy, female domestic shorthair, deceased at time of conversation
Tabs, female domestic shorthair, age 10

BIRDS

Brandy, female cockatiel, age 7

GOATS

Buddy, male myotonic (fainting) goat, age 10, since deceased
Lily, female myotonic (fainting) goat, age 10, since deceased

HORSES

Bucks Arrow, Thoroughbred gelding, age 11
Luna Belle, Andalusian-Arabian mare, age 13
Northern Hawk, off-track Thoroughbred gelding, age 7

∽

FAMILY GROUPS

Collective of five pet siblings: Lola, April, Buttercup, Marcy, and Sparky
Collective of five dog siblings: Shadow, Jasmine, Leo, Phoenix, and Sage
Collective of four cat siblings: Pixie, Sage, Luna, and Neo

ACKNOWLEDGMENTS

Facilitating conversations with members of the animal kingdom brings me great joy, and I am humbled and honored to do so. However, all kudos belong to my partner and soulmate, Will, without whom this book would not be possible. He is the bridge to the energy of the animals we speak with. It is his selfless surrender and implicit trust in his guides that allow for this miracle of communication to take place.

Immense love and gratitude goes out to all of the animals we've communicated with, who consistently offer their wisdom and advice with no expectation of anything in return.

I am thankful for my own pet-teachers, Comet, Dasher, and Oliver, who have helped me reach greater levels of compassion than I thought possible, as well as Buddy and Lily who continue to assist us from across the veil.

I also owe a debt of gratitude to all of the pet parents who graciously allowed me to share their pets' beautiful words with the world.

I am blessed with some of the most amazing friends on the planet, but there are two, in particular, who are always willing to read and critique my manuscripts: Judy Buchanan and Donna Kennedy. Love you both!

Thank you, Candace Craw Goldman, for so many things...your friendship and generosity, bringing Beyond Quantum Healing (BQH) to the planet, and for tutoring me in horse lingo!

Special thanks to Samantha Carver who graciously transcribes our monthly channeling sessions—you are so appreciated!

Thank you, Donna McMurtry and Diana Adair, primarily for your unwavering love and support but also for helping me navigate my first self-publishing experience.

Speaking of self-publishing...even though there is a lot of leg work, I have absolutely loved being able to express my creativity through the design process! That being said, there were some key players that helped make this book a success—my fantastic transcriptionist, Madeleine (Fiverr), cover designer Shahbail Shabbir (99Designs), and all of my Facebook friends, who helped solidify the title and select the final cover.

Thank you, Barbara Becker, for your consistent support of your friends and colleagues.

In closing, Will and I would like to express our deep gratitude for all of the pet parents who have, over the past several years, trusted us to facilitate communication with their beloved animals. It has been such an amazing adventure! We are blessed beyond measure.

ABOUT THE AUTHOR

Dr. Allison Brown is a best-selling author, educator, and quantum healer. Her first book, *The Journey Within: A Christian's Guide to 14 Non-traditional Spiritual Practices*, is an inspiring and courageous account of her search for reconciliation between a newfound spirituality and her traditional Christian upbringing. Allison's second book, a collaborative effort entitled *The Ancestor's Within: Reveal and Heal the Ancient Memories You Carry*, offers a wide-range of heart-centered stories and actionable practices for those seeking ancestral healing and connection.

As a Reiki Master and a Quantum Healing Practitioner, Allison employs a spiritual hypnosis modality called Beyond Quantum Healing (BQH). Holding a master's degree in counseling psychology and a doctorate in educational leadership, Allison's use of metaphysical practices within a framework of traditional counseling gives her the unique ability to gently uncover and address her clients' underlying issues.

Find out more about Allison's books and services at www. drallisonbrown.com

William (Will) Brown, is a psychic medium, trance channel, and Reiki Master. Serving as a guinea pig during his wife's Reiki training in 2014 reawakened the spirit connection he had sensed throughout his childhood but had been too busy to contemplate during his twenty-six

years with the Coast Guard. Will has since realized his passion and purpose as a healer, teacher, and messenger.

Holding a bachelor's degree in workforce education and development and a master's degree in project management, Will had worked in the start-up world since retiring from the Coast Guard in 2014. But in early 2018, a chance encounter with a QHHT® practitioner put him in touch with his spiritual team, a group of loving beings that call themselves The Collective. Since that time, Will has brought their messages of love to folks all over the world.

Will and Allison reside in Moncks Corner, South Carolina with their two children, two cats, and a rooster.

You can read more about Will on his website, www.william-brown.com

To schedule a pet channeling, visit www.palmandlotus.com

In 2016 Will and Allison, both veterans, founded Reiki for Vets (RFV), a non-profit organization that provides free Reiki clinics under the auspices of the Veteran's Administration. RFV also provides scholarships to veterans and their spouses to obtain their Reiki Level 1 certification.

Learn more about Reiki for Vets at www.reikiforvets.org

www.ingramcontent.com/pod-product-compliance
Lightning Source LLC
Chambersburg PA
CBHW071149130626
46553CB00004B/1587